THE PRINCIPLE OF BECOMING

Three Essential Prerequisites For The Journey to Destiny Fulfillment

Yeshua S. Jehu

Yeshua S. Jehu

Appreciation

To God Almighty, who in His infinite grace has granted me divine revelations, timely resources, strengthening counsel, and unwavering guidance through every season. I give profound thanks for His abundant wisdom, faithfulness, and sovereign hand that has sustained, inspired, and carried this work from inception to completion. All glory belongs to Him alone.

Contents

THE PRINCIPLE OF BECOMING

THREE PREREQUISITES

1 **Primal Consecration**

2. **Sacrifice**

3. **Anointing: Divine Appointment**

Vision for the Book

Every generation faces a defining call—to rise, to mature, and to answer the destiny imprinted on their very souls. This book, *The Principle of Becoming,* is born out of that call. Its vision is simple yet eternal: to illuminate the divine process by which ordinary men and women are forged into vessels of extraordinary purpose in the hands of God. Within these pages, you will uncover the patterns that unlock destiny, the rhythms that shape becoming, and the sacred tools to move intentionally into the fullness of your calling.

Preface

Have you ever wondered why some lives seem to unfold with prophetic inevitability—marked by transformation, power, and divine influence—while others linger in the shadows of unfulfilled potential? Scripture is filled with many whose stories echo a consistent, divine order—a principle that sets the stage for destiny.

The purpose of this book is to uncover that principle, to make it visible, tangible, and accessible—to those who dare to become intentional participants in the sacred journey God has ordained for all who belong to Him. In the chapters that follow, we will explore not merely what it means *to become*, but *how* that becoming unfolds in the hands of the Potter. Each stage is a holy prerequisite for the next, and only by embracing all three does one enter into the fullness of mature sonship.

"By the mouth of two or three witnesses the matter shall be established" (Deuteronomy 19:15, NKJV). This is the law of divine validation—the principle of final judgment.

Every pattern story given, every pattern bearer whose life we examine within these pages, stands as a witness. Together, they form an unbroken chain of evidence revealing the immutable truth of this sacred principle. You will see that it remains the very pattern by which our gracious Creator still raises, refines, and releases His servants to advance His Kingdom in every generation. Should you heed the call and yield faithfully to the journey of becoming, then you too—like those whose lives bear the eternal imprint of this divine principle—will *Become.*

Foundational Truths About Principles

Before delving further, it is vital to understand a few immutable truths about principles themselves:

• Principles Are Predictable

The outcome of any true principle is determined at its origin. The seed already contains its harvest. When you learn to discern divine principles, you gain spiritual foresight—you can measure your present and anticipate your future by the pattern you obey. For every principle carries within it a prophecy, and its end is as certain as its beginning.

• Principles Are Proven by Repetition

Repetition is the signature of truth. If a pattern produces results again and again—whether in Scripture or in life—it bears witness to the operation of an established principle. Throughout this book, we will trace *The Principle of Becoming*—tested and proven through the lives of those I call *Pattern Bearers*: individuals whose consistent journeys reveal this divine process in motion. Their stories are not random events; they are prophetic templates. They reached the fullness of their destinies because they aligned with this principle, knowingly or not.

• Principles Are Unbiased

Ninety-nine percent of biblical principles function with impartial consistency for anyone who applies them, irrespective of spiritual standing. Just as the rain falls on both the righteous and the unrighteous, and a seed sown will grow for any farmer, so divine principles produce for all who obey their order.

As Jesus said, *"For the sons of this world are more shrewd in their generation than the sons of light"* (Luke 16:8, NIV).

However, there remains a sacred one percent—principles reserved for citizens of the Kingdom. These are not universal laws; they are covenantal secrets, inherited by those who are born of the Spirit, heirs of salvation. The *Principle of Becoming* belongs to this category. Every Pattern Bearer in Scripture was a covenant person, for only Kingdom citizens can inherit the full measure of what this principle promises.

• Principles Transcend Context

One profound reality I have discovered about the governing principles of life is this: a true principle cannot be confined. Its power extends beyond circumstance, culture, and time. Shift your perspective, alter the lens through which you view it, and another facet of its glory unfolds before you.

This is why the Bible—the eternal Creator's manual—remains ever potent and perpetually relevant. The secret of its timelessness lies in the fact that every divine principle within it transcends the scene that first revealed it. The story may be bound by history, but the principle breathes with eternity.

Thus, apply every principle you learn beyond the context in which you first discovered it, and you will unearth countless treasures of wisdom. Each revelation becomes a key to dominion in another dimension of life.

Remember, in this age of overwhelming information, wisdom is gold—and he who holds the gold, governs. Therefore, seek understanding; stay ahead of the curve; and let revelation become your wealth.

Some may appear to have reached fullness by worldly standards—through wealth, achievement, or stature—yet remain impoverished toward God. True destiny fullness, in the eyes of Heaven, is not measured by outward success but by inward maturity, obedience, and divine alignment with His eternal purpose.

Throughout Scripture, there were men such as the rich fool, who amassed abundance but failed to become *"rich toward God"* (Luke 12:21, NIV). Our Pattern Bearers, by contrast, were brought into destiny's fullness not for personal acclaim, but as *first-fruits*—living offerings for the sake of generations yet unborn, for a people divinely linked to their obedience (Romans 8:18–21, NIV).

To *become* in the Kingdom is to answer the cry of creation itself for liberty and for light. Humanity groans beneath the weight of corruption and darkness (Romans 8:19–21, NIV; Isaiah 60:1–2, NIV). Yet those who arise to walk this sacred path become vessels through whom God releases freedom, illumination, and restoration into the earth. *"Arise, shine, for your light has come, and the glory of the LORD rises upon you..."* (Isaiah 60:1, NIV).

Believer, destiny is never solely about you; both failure and success ripple through the generations tied to your purpose.

In the Kingdom, promotion is never granted without proof. One must demonstrate readiness for elevation, for just as in earthly systems competence must be proven, so in the divine order the *King* will not risk the innocent under the stewardship of one found lax or unfaithful. The Sovereign entrusts responsibility only to the proven, to those refined by faithfulness and fire.

Thus, the journey to *become* is reserved for the resolute—for those determined to walk the path all the way to fullness. If you will pursue it with unwavering resolve, *The Principle of Becoming* will not fail you.

This book exists to give you perspective and clarity for each step—to equip you to measure progress and calibrate your walk with wisdom and insight. God's pattern is woven subtly yet unmistakably throughout Scripture, revealed in the lives of the *Pattern Bearers* and their *Pattern Stories.*

And you will see—through the unblinking lens of Scripture—that at the culmination of every life faithfully carried through this process of becoming, one divine result is constant: the advancement of the Kingdom of God, the deliverance and salvation of souls, and the manifestation of His glory acknowledged even by the most unlikely.

At the final prerequisite lies a greatness unlike anything attainable by the carnal. It is both spiritual and practical—an endowment of divine power and influence bestowed upon the faithful, that they might execute even greater works for the Kingdom of God.

Becoming as a Biblical Principle

From Genesis to Revelation, the *Principle of Becoming* weaves through the tapestry of Scripture—tracing the divine transformation of men and women who yielded to God's process. From Abraham to Joseph, from Moses to Esther, from David to the disciples and the apostle Paul, the same sequence resounds: **calling, consecration, sacrifice, and divine appointment.**

We shall follow these Pattern Bearers in chronological order—from the first glimpse of this principle unveiled in the Old Testament, to its perfected expression in the New. Over and over again, the pages of Scripture testify: destiny is never accidental. Those who *became* were not shaped by chance, but by a deliberate divine order—a process meticulously orchestrated by the hand of God Himself.

This is more than a historical pattern; it is a living summons. For even now, the world groans beneath its need for sons and daughters who have come into the fullness of their becoming—God's firstfruits, mature and ready to bear His image into a darkened age.

Creation waits with expectation for such as these: those who will arise as carriers of light, healers of nations, restorers of divine order. The *Principle of Becoming* remains Heaven's chosen path to raise them.

This book is your map for that sacred journey—an unveiling of the process that turns ordinary vessels into divine instruments, that you too might *become* all God ordained from the beginning of time.

PREREQUISITE ONE: PRIMAL CONSECRATION

Introduction to Primal Consecration

Consecration means being *set apart*—separated from the ordinary, reserved for a divine cause, sanctified for the purposes of God. The *primal consecration* I speak of here refers to the foundational season in a believer's journey—the sacred beginning where spiritual formation takes root and the believer begins to grow into fullness in the Word of God. It is the phase where one learns to walk with maturity, anchored in prayer, rooted in truth, and cleansed of the remnants of the world's influence.

This initial season is vital. It establishes the believer's rhythm of devotion—building a functional prayer life, grounding them in the Word, breaking the chains of worldly attachments, confronting generational or foundational bondages, and purging the soul from hidden iniquities. It is the stage where the believer casts off weights and hindrances, and by the fire of the Spirit, is purified in Christ.

When this season is neglected or incomplete, future ministry, sacrifices, and service often carry "chaff"—the residue of impurity that contaminates the offering. In divine terms, such a person's *wine* is mixed, their *grain offering* still laden with husks. The fragrance of their service is marred by mixture.

Thus, consecration precedes and guarantees the quality and acceptance of sacrifice before God. It is the refining that ensures the vessel is worthy of what Heaven will pour.

Biblical Roots and Importance of Consecration

In the Old Testament, purification was always the precondition for divine acceptance. Every sacrifice had to be cleansed, every vessel purified, every priest sanctified before entering the Holy Place.

For example, burnt offerings were first washed with water before being placed on the altar (Leviticus 1:9). Though Christ has fulfilled the ceremonial laws, these rituals unveiled an eternal truth—the divine principle that purity and holiness must precede offering.

To offer what is unclean before a holy God is to invite rejection. Such an offering violates the sanctity of His nature, for the Lord will not receive what has not been first refined.

The apostle Paul echoes this same truth, warning that *"each one's work will become clear; for the Day will declare it, because it will be revealed by fire"* (1 Corinthians 3:13, NKJV). Those who have not purified themselves through consecration will see their works consumed in that testing flame.

This is the spiritual danger of entering ministry—or any sacrificial service—without first passing through the waters of consecration. For where there is no purification, there can be no permanence; and where there is no consecration, there can be no true commission.

The Danger of Skipping Consecration: The Example of Solomon

A striking example of the danger of bypassing consecration is found in Solomon—one who was empowered by God before being fully sanctified as his father David was. Though Solomon excelled in sacrifice (prerequisite two), *(1 Kings 3:4–5)* and received God's blessing, the absence of full *primal consecration* left him open to corruption and eventual spiritual decline.

Solomon's story is a solemn warning that God desires to anoint *mature sons*—those whose hearts have been purified through consecration before elevation. The absence of consecration breeds instability. Power without purity corrupts, and influence without intimacy with God leads to downfall.

While principles may appear to operate partially even without full consecration, divine trust and enduring authority rest only upon those who have been wholly set apart. Heaven's endorsement is not granted to the gifted but to the purified. *"An inheritance gained hastily at the beginning will not be blessed at the end"* (Proverbs 20:21 NKJV).

Premature empowerment is dangerous—it invites spiritual collapse and endangers the people entrusted to one's care. Without consecration, one may function in gifting yet drift into deception, becoming what the Lord calls *"a worker of iniquity"*—active in service, yet unknown in intimacy. *(Matthew 7:23)*

Purpose and Keys to Consecration

Consecration is born out of purpose. It begins as an act of faith and devotion—a decisive step of surrender that declares, *'I am Yours, Lord, for Your purpose alone.'*

Scripture consistently anchors this truth: purity and holiness are the non-negotiable prerequisites for effective ministry *"I looked for a man among them who would build up the wall and stand before me in the gap on behalf of the land so I would not have to destroy it, but I found none."* Ezekiel 22:30 (NIV).

God calls us to be vessels of honour—usable, sanctified, and free from defilement.

Meditation on the Word of God lies at the heart of consecration. Through meditation, we commune with His precepts, recall His testimonies, and rehearse His mighty works. We ponder His victories, promises, and dealings—until His truth saturates our being. This sacred discipline tames the flesh, renews the mind, and fortifies the spirit.

Prayer, worship, and meditation are the triune cords by which consecration is maintained. Through them, we remain aligned, sensitive, and yielded.

True dedication to spiritual maturity demands balance—the harmony between the **kingly** and **priestly** dimensions within us. The **kingly** nature governs, leads, and stewards faithfully the work of our hands—the responsibilities and dominions entrusted to us. The **priestly** nature worships, intercedes, and walks in holiness—nurturing prayer, studying the Word, growing in spiritual stature, and becoming a covering, a watchman proven by faithfulness.

Consecration is, therefore, not passivity—it is the faith step that proves belief in God's ability to fulfill His promises, even when our strength falters. It is active surrender—obedience that builds capacity for glory. Only those who are first *consecrated* can be safely *commissioned*.

Levels of Spiritual Maturity in the Journey to Become

Understanding consecration requires knowing the stages of spiritual maturity, described with Greek terms that mirror human development:

• **NEPIOS (Νήπιος)** — *Spiritual infancy,* marked by immaturity and dependence. At this stage, the believer is easily swayed, still learning to discern the Shepherd's voice, and dependent on others for spiritual sustenance.

• **PAIDION (Παιδίον)** — *Early childhood of faith,* marked by humility and the beginnings of understanding. The believer begins to respond to divine instruction and walk in simple obedience but is still developing discernment and endurance.

• **TEKNON (Τέκνον)** — *Older childhood/apprenticeship in faith.* This stage mirrors spiritual adolescence—a believer learning to apply God's Word and gifts with growing consistency and conviction. Here, they begin to partner with the Spirit, yet still require shaping and correction to handle responsibility with grace. *(Spiritual teenagers.)*

• **NEANISKOS (Νεανίσκος)** — *Youth, young adult.* This is the youngest stage at which one is truly mature enough to intentionally begin the journey of becoming. At this level, believers live by the deliberate application of God's Word—they read, meditate, and align their lives consistently with divine truth. They love deeply, walk in purity, and make choices rooted in conviction rather than convenience.

They are no longer tossed by emotions or worldliness; they are anchored in Christ, motivated by an inner desire for transformation and holiness. Their faith becomes intentional, their pursuit relentless, and their focus refined. No longer passive spectators in the faith—they become active participants who consciously partner with the Spirit in the process of growth. This is the stage where consecration truly begins to manifest fruit.

• **HUIOS (Υἱός)** — *Fathers; mature sonship.* This is the place of full maturity—where one walks in the authority, love, and likeness of the Father. The *huios* is led by the Spirit in all things, embodying the heart and will of God on earth. This level marks the believer's entrance into divine trust and stewardship. Here, one can raise others, lead with integrity, and bear fruit that remains. It is the dimension expected of those whom God calls into deeper partnership and leadership in His Kingdom. Only at this stage—this fullness of maturity—can one be entrusted to advance into the final prerequisite of becoming.

These stages reflect progressive growth toward Christlikeness, each one enlarging the believer's capacity to carry revelation, responsibility, and power. The *Neaniskos* stage, however, stands as the critical threshold where faith transitions from dependence to discipline—from inspiration to intentionality. It is here that the believer's character is refined, and their vessel prepared for greater measures of glory.

As *Proverbs 20:21 (NKJV)* declares, *"An inheritance gained hastily at the beginning will not be blessed at the end."* It is God's mercy that withholds overflow until capacity is built. To bypass this process is to forfeit stability; but to yield to it is to secure longevity in divine purpose.

The Significance of Completing Prerequisite One

Consecration is the gateway to becoming a vessel chosen and trusted by God. It is the divine filter that separates the common from the consecrated, the willing from the worthy. Before the High Priest could enter the Most Holy Place, he was required to perform a ritual purification every year (*Leviticus 16*). This act was more than ceremony—it was prophetic, revealing that no man approaches divine appointment without first being sanctified by divine process.

Without sufficient consecration, ministry or anointing remains incomplete and subject to rejection. God's standards are not negotiable; He demands distinction between what is holy and what is common. As written, *"Do not drink wine or intoxicating drink... that you may distinguish between holy and unholy, and between unclean and clean"* (*Leviticus 10:9–10, NKJV*). Likewise, *"Let the priests who come near the LORD consecrate themselves, lest the LORD break out against them"* (*Exodus 19:22, NKJV*).

To skip consecration is to risk collapse under the weight of calling. To complete it is to be refined for purpose—to become a vessel through which God's presence may safely dwell and His power freely flow. Only then can one enter the fullness of divine purpose, not as a novice standing near the sacred, but as one proven faithful to stand within it.

PATTERN BEARERS: Biblical Examples of Primal Consecration Applied

Many Are Called, But Few Are Chosen

"For many are called, but few are chosen." — Matthew 22:14 (NKJV)

To reach the realm of the *chosen* requires consecration. Calling may introduce you to divine purpose, but consecration refines and qualifies you for it. The biblical characters we will examine as **Pattern Bearers** are individuals who journeyed through all three prerequisites—**Primal Consecration**, **Sacrifice**, and **Anointing: Divine Appointment**—to reach the fullness of what God intended for them.

In this section, we will look closely at their beginnings—their initial consecration—and how they embarked on the sacred path to becoming. Through their journeys, we will uncover lessons, warnings, and divine wisdom to help you, dear reader, avoid pitfalls and align yourself accurately in your own process of becoming.

Each Pattern Bearer's story offers unique nuances and vital insights necessary for spiritual growth and destiny fulfillment. As we examine their lives step by step, prerequisite by prerequisite, we will unveil not only the evidence of this principle but also a **functional blueprint** for your personal application and transformation.

Principle and Pattern: Foundations of Spiritual Growth

Before proceeding, it is essential to understand that consistent biblical patterns reveal *true spiritual principles*. Repetition is divine endorsement. What God does once is revelation; what He repeats becomes law. Thus,

"The Principle of the Prerequisites of the Journey to Become," or simply, "The Principle of Becoming," stands as an immutable truth—it is God's established method for shaping and approving His chosen vessels.

As the Scripture declares, *"By the mouth of two or three witnesses every word shall be established." — 2 Corinthians 13:1 (NKJV)*

This is the **Law of Final Judgment**—the divine confirmation that the pattern seen across multiple lives is no coincidence, but the sovereign design of God for all who are called to *become.*

PATTERN BEARERS: PREREQUISITE ONE

ABRAM: The First Pattern Bearer

The Call of Abram

Genesis 12:1–3 (NIV) The LORD said to Abram, "Go from your country, your people and your father's household to the land I will show you. I will make you into a great nation, and I will bless you; I will make your name great, and you will be a blessing. I will bless those who bless you, and whoever curses you I will curse; and all peoples on earth will be blessed through you."

Here, we encounter the first unveiling of the Principle of Becoming—the divine summons to consecration. God's words to Abram were not merely an invitation to relocation but a command to separation: *"Go from your country, your people, and your father's household."* This was the first act of consecration—the **Primal Consecration**—the breaking away from the familiar to follow the invisible.

Every true journey toward destiny begins with this call: *"Leave what you have known, that I may make you what I have designed."* Abram's obedience to depart from Ur marked the birth of a process that would culminate in transformation. Only after answering the call to be set apart does the journey to greatness begin.

To *"make you into a great nation"* is a divine promise anchored in process. Before one can become a vessel of blessing, one must first become *separate.* Abram's story sets the precedent for all Pattern Bearers: **Consecration precedes exaltation.**

Only after Abram embraced this sacred separation did God transition him into prerequisite two—Sacrifice. There, through the offering of covenant and obedience, Abram became *Abraham.* This change of name was not cosmetic—it signified transformation by covenant, a shift from promise to purpose, from calling to commission. His obedience in consecration became the womb through which his divine appointment would one day manifest.

The Covenant of Circumcision: Walking Blamelessly

Genesis 17:1–14 (NIV) "When Abram was ninety-nine years old, the Lord appeared to him and said, 'I am God Almighty; walk before Me faithfully and be blameless. Then I will make My covenant between Me and you and will greatly increase your numbers...'"

This divine charge unveils the very essence of Prerequisite One—to *walk faithfully and blamelessly before God.* Consecration is not a momentary event; it is a sustained walk of separation, a continual choosing of God over the world, of obedience over compromise. Through the covenant of circumcision, God established a physical and spiritual seal of distinction between His chosen and the rest of mankind—a mark that set His people apart unto Himself.

This command embodies the heart of Primal Consecration—to live untouched by the world's corruption and free from the dominion of the sinful nature. It is the stage of *Neaniskos* maturity, where the believer intentionally chooses holiness, walking in faithfulness and spiritual discipline. It is at this level that one becomes equipped to begin the journey of *becoming* with clarity and endurance.

The Apostle Paul expands this mystery in his letter to the Romans, revealing that the true circumcision God now requires is inward and spiritual—the consecration of the heart by the Spirit of God.

Romans 2:28–29 (NIV) "A person is not a Jew who is one only outwardly, nor is circumcision merely outward and physical. No, a person is a Jew who is one inwardly; and circumcision is circumcision of the heart, by the Spirit, not by the written code. Such a person's praise is not from other people, but from God."

This revelation unveils the deeper dimension of consecration in the New Covenant: it is no longer the cutting of the flesh, but the circumcision of the heart—the removal of inner impurity, pride, and rebellion. It is the Spirit's transforming work that renews the believer from within, aligning the heart to God's will and empowering a blameless walk before Him.

Thus, through Abram, we see the divine continuity of this principle: the **call to leave**, the **covenant to live**, and the **consecration to last**—first established outwardly in the Old Testament, and now fulfilled inwardly by the Spirit in the New. This eternal pattern forms the immovable foundation for every true journey of *becoming*.

The Neaniskos Stage: The Gateway to Intentional Becoming

At *Neaniskos*, believers have cultivated the spiritual maturity to live life by applying God's Word intentionally. They are not new believers ignorant of truth, nor are they yet mature sons fully seasoned in Christ. They stand at the threshold—young adults in spiritual strength—who consistently seek to break free from worldly influence and no longer live to please people but God alone.

They possess a heart freed from the demands of fleshly desires, recognizing these as obstacles to growth. Their faith is purposeful, their dedication genuine, and their appetite for growth unquenchable. They have the focus, discipline, and resolve needed to engage the journey fully—this maturity best equips them to commence the journey of becoming because they live by applicable principles, rooted in God's Word and intentional obedience.

In essence, *Neaniskos* is not just a stage of survival; it is the launching point for transformation. Those at this stage have chosen to embrace the full process of consecration and are prepared to face the challenges ahead.

Moving Toward Covenant: Preparing for Sacrifice

Abraham's example shows that walking blamelessly and faithfully (prerequisite one) leads to covenant relationship with God (prerequisite two). At this stage, believers realize there is no life outside God's purposes and are willing to sacrifice even that which is dear to them to advance the journey.

In subsequent chapters, we will explore how Abraham—and many others—navigate sacrifices that cement their covenant walk, preparing them for divine appointment (anointing) and ultimate destiny.

JACOB: The Alignment of Identity

Instruments of Divine Transfer: God's Movers in the Journey

As we continue exploring the Pattern Bearers of Prerequisite One—*Primal Consecration*—we introduce the concept of *Instruments of Divine Transfer*. These are individuals God uses to move you from one stage of the journey to the next, regardless of their relationship to you. Whether friend or foe, their role is vital and divinely ordained to advance your destiny. Scripture establishes that matters are confirmed by the testimony of two or three witnesses: *"One witness shall not rise against a man concerning any iniquity or any sin that he commits; by the mouth of two or three witnesses the matter shall be established"* (Deuteronomy 19:15, NKJV).

The lives of these pattern bearers collectively testify to this truth: God sovereignly orchestrates circumstances and people to ensure His purpose. You cannot argue with facts.

The Story of Jacob: Divine Orchestration in Action

Jacob's journey exemplifies the role of instruments of divine transfer in shaping the path of consecration. From the very beginning, God had a clear agenda for Jacob's life—even before birth—instructing Rebekah about the struggles in her womb and the destinies of her twins: *"And the LORD said to her: 'Two nations are in your womb, two peoples shall be separated from your body; one people shall be stronger than the other, and the older shall serve the younger'"* (Genesis 25:23, NKJV).

This divine purpose was far beyond simple family drama. Esau's vengeful rage became the instrument God used to send Jacob away from his father Isaac's household.

Rebekah, compelled by wisdom and divine insight, urged Jacob to flee to her brother Laban's household: Esau had said in his heart, *"'The days of mourning for my father are at hand; then I will kill my brother Jacob.' And the words of Esau her older son were told to Rebekah. So she sent and called Jacob her younger son, and said to him, 'Surely your brother Esau comforts himself concerning you by intending to kill you. Now therefore, my son, obey my voice: arise, flee to my brother Laban in Haran'"* (Genesis 27:41–43, NKJV).

Here, amid manipulation and hardship, Jacob began his season of primal consecration.

Primal Consecration in Laban's Household

Jacob's exile was no mere coincidence, but an orchestrated journey to break him and set him apart. Living with Laban, who repeatedly cheated and challenged him, Jacob was being refined. This crucible shaped him from a self-reliant son into a man dependent on God's promises—dedicated to a higher purpose.

During this season, Jacob married Leah and Rachel, and fathered children who would become foundational to Israel's twelve tribes. These were not accidental blessings but divine tools prepared for his national destiny.

The Promise and the Personal Encounter

Before reaching Laban, Jacob had an intimate encounter with God at Bethel, where he dreamed of a ladder reaching heaven and received promises of God's presence and blessing:

"Then he dreamed, and behold, a ladder was set up on the earth, and its top reached to heaven; and there the angels of God were ascending and descending on it. And behold, the LORD stood above it and said: 'I am the LORD God of Abraham your father and the God of Isaac; the land on which you lie I will give to you and your descendants. Also your descendants shall be as the dust of the earth; you shall spread abroad to the west and the east, to the north and the south; and in you and in your seed all the families of the earth shall be blessed. Behold, I am with you and will keep you wherever you go, and will bring you back to this land; for I will not leave you until I have done what I have spoken to you'" (Genesis 28:12–15, NKJV).

Jacob awoke in awe and declared, *"Surely the LORD is in this place, and I did not know it... This is none other than the house of God, and this is the gate of heaven!"* (Genesis 28:16–17, NKJV). He then vowed, *"If God will be with me, and keep me in this way that I am going, and give me bread to eat and clothing to put on, so that I come back to my father's house in peace, then the LORD shall be my God. And this stone which I have set as a pillar shall be God's house, and of all that You give me I will surely give a tenth to You"* (Genesis 28:20–22, NKJV).

This encounter transformed Jacob's faith from inherited belief to personal conviction, grounding him in a vision for his destiny. Yet, despite moving toward promise, Jacob still bore an unrefined character—a name meaning 'supplanter,' reflecting struggle and deceit. Consecration is about transformation; he was set apart but still being purified.

The Clash and the Change: Wrestling with God

Years later, as Jacob returned home to claim the land promised to his grandfather Abraham, God met him in a climactic encounter of wrestling:

"Then Jacob was left alone; and a Man wrestled with him until the breaking of day. Now when He saw that He did not prevail against him, He touched the socket of his hip; and the socket of Jacob's hip was out of joint as He wrestled with Him. And He said, 'Let Me go, for the day breaks.' But he said, 'I will not let You go unless You bless me!' So He said to him, 'What is your name?' He said, 'Jacob.' And He said, 'Your name shall no longer be called Jacob, but Israel; for you have struggled with God and with men, and have prevailed'" (Genesis 32:24–28, NKJV).

This was not merely physical—it was a divine confrontation that exposed Jacob's heart and purified his destiny. God dislocated his hip, leaving him with a permanent limp—a reminder of divine breaking that precedes divine becoming.

God's renaming of Jacob to *Israel*—meaning "he who prevails with God"—signified the stripping away of the old and the revelation of the ordained identity. Scripture later confirms this transition: *"Then God appeared to Jacob again, when he came from Padan Aram, and blessed him. And God said to him, 'Your name is Jacob; your name shall not be called Jacob anymore, but Israel shall be your name.' So He called his name Israel. Also God said to him: 'I am God Almighty. Be fruitful and multiply; a nation and a company of nations shall proceed from you, and kings shall come from your body. The land which I gave Abraham and Isaac I give to you; and to your descendants after you I give this land'"* (Genesis 35:9–12, NKJV).

This divine affirmation sealed Jacob's consecration. The name *Israel* was his rightful inheritance—ordained from eternity. This truth is echoed in God's prophetic dealings: every chosen vessel bears a name tied to eternal purpose (Isaiah 49:1).

Just as Jacob refused to let go until blessed, this moment illustrates the perseverance required in consecration. Impurities—such as misplaced identity, pride, or self-reliance—must be discarded before advancing to the next prerequisite.

The Importance of Primal Consecration

Jacob's journey reminds us that skipping or inadequately completing this first prerequisite invites divine correction—a humbling essential for true advancement. *"Therefore humble yourselves under the mighty hand of God, that He may exalt you in due time"* (1 Peter 5:6, NKJV).

Just as the High Priests of old had to fully complete the rites of consecration before entering the Most Holy Place, so must we finish our season of being set apart before moving forward. Though the rituals were temporal, the principles of God that governed them remain eternal.

Jacob's time in consecration was preparation for the next stage—*Sacrifice*—where complete surrender would be demanded. Only after his heart was purified and identity realigned could he safely enter covenant promises and divine appointment.

God's instruction for Jacob to return and claim the promise made to Abraham *(Genesis 35:9–12)* marked the end of one season and the threshold of another. This divine mandate demonstrates that consecration always precedes fulfillment.

Jacob's story, like Abraham's before him, teaches us the paramount importance of *Primal Consecration*: being broken, purified, and set apart to align fully with God's will before the journey of becoming truly unfolds.

JOSEPH: Set Apart from the Start

From the very beginning, Joseph stood as the cherished jewel of his father's household—a young man in his element and seemingly in a comfort zone. Gifted with the *coat of many colors*, a symbol of distinction and future leadership within their culture, Joseph was clearly marked as the heir apparent of his family's legacy.

Yet God's plan reached far beyond familial honor. Joseph was destined to become a faithful steward—a vessel through whom God would preserve nations and secure His covenant lineage. To fulfill this divine purpose, God employed Joseph's own brothers as *Instruments of Divine Transfer*—those appointed to orchestrate painful yet purposeful movements essential to his journey.

Consecration through Tribulation: The Beginning of the Journey

The betrayal by his brothers and his sale into slavery marked the critical transition into Joseph's *Primal Consecration*. Torn from his home and comfort, Joseph entered a divine separation—the first refining fire. This stage stripped him of privilege and reliance on family favor, leaving only faith to anchor him.

God was setting him apart through hardship. What appeared as rejection was, in truth, redirection. Joseph's isolation became incubation. The Lord was forming a steward fit for global responsibility—one tested, proven, and purified in private before being exalted in public.

It is vital to recognize that in the journey to *become*, one never outgrows any prerequisite. Instead, we continually deepen them. Consecration remains a lifelong posture of yieldedness—a living sacrifice continually refined by God *(Romans 12:1)*.

Transitioning Toward Sacrifice

When Joseph was purchased by Potiphar, captain of Pharaoh's guard, a new phase began. *"Now Joseph had been taken down to Egypt. And Potiphar, an officer of Pharaoh, captain of the guard, an Egyptian, bought him from the Ishmaelites who had taken him down there. The LORD was with Joseph, and he was a successful man; and he was in the house of his master the Egyptian"* (Genesis 39:1–2, NKJV).

Here, Joseph's consecration matured into disciplined stewardship. Despite his circumstance, he served faithfully and excellently—his faith in God producing fruit even in captivity. This stage signaled movement toward the next prerequisite—*Sacrifice*—where obedience costs more and tests deepen.

Potiphar's house became a proving ground. In that environment, Joseph learned to serve without recognition and to lead without title. Every act of faithfulness refined him for divine elevation.

A Heart Free of Bitterness

Remarkably, Joseph harbored no bitterness toward his brothers. His heart, purified through the fires of consecration, had been freed from vengeance. When tested, he chose forgiveness over fury and perspective over pain. His words to his brothers later confirmed this divine maturity: *"But as for you,*

you meant evil against me; but God meant it for good, in order to bring it about as it is this day, to save many people alive" (Genesis 50:20, NKJV).

Such words could only come from one fully yielded to God's sovereignty. The man once adorned in multicolored favor now wore the invisible garment of meekness and divine wisdom. His consecration had produced character strong enough to carry destiny without corruption.

Joseph's journey affirms that consecration is not avoidance of pain, but transformation through it. Every betrayal, pit, and prison became a step toward palace purpose. Through Joseph, we see that consecration refines character, purges the heart of bitterness, and positions the believer for divine stewardship.

His life stands as a timeless truth: **those whom God sets apart, He first strips apart**—removing comfort, pride, and familiarity until what remains is a vessel fit for His glory.

Joseph's progression from *favored son* to *faithful servant* illustrates the Principle of Becoming—where separation precedes elevation, and consecration prepares the soul to sustain destiny's weight.

MOSES: Consecration in the Wilderness

Moses' journey into consecration began dramatically with his flight from Pharaoh after killing an Egyptian. Though this act appeared impulsive, it was divinely orchestrated—a move of providence through what can be termed an *Instrument of Divine Transfer.* God used this crisis to sever Moses from the Egyptian identity, mindset, and affiliations that had shaped him as a prince in Pharaoh's house.

The wilderness became Moses' furnace of formation—the place of *Primal Consecration*. Stripped of luxury, position, and recognition, Moses entered a divine reset where his dependence on human systems was exchanged for reliance upon God. This forty-year exile in Midian was no punishment but preparation, a season of holy separation designed to purge Egypt out of him before God could bring Israel out of Egypt.

Scripture recounts: *"One day, after Moses had grown up, he went out to where his own people were and watched them at their hard labor. He saw an Egyptian beating a Hebrew, one of his own people. Looking this way and that and seeing no one, he killed the Egyptian and hid him in the sand."* (Exodus 2:11–12, NIV)

When the matter became known and Pharaoh sought to kill him, Moses fled to Midian *(Exodus 2:15).* There, his identity as an Egyptian prince was dismantled piece by piece. Every trace of worldly stature, education, and self-reliance was stripped away. He who once wore the robes of royalty now tended sheep in obscurity. Yet in God's design, this humility was not a demotion but a divine transition into *Primal Consecration*—the first prerequisite of the journey to *become.*

Here, all Egyptian ties were severed; his princely plaques revoked, his name redefined by solitude. Moses was precisely where God wanted him: hidden, humbled, and being honed. After forty years—the fullness of divine timing for his consecration—the LORD appeared to him in the burning bush, marking his graduation from separation to commission *(Exodus 3:1–12).*

In that sacred encounter, God revealed His Name, His purpose, and Moses' assignment—to deliver His people from bondage. The man who fled Egypt in fear would return as the instrument of God's deliverance.

The Threshold of Righteousness: The Circumcision Crisis

Though Moses had endured his season of separation, one critical aspect of consecration remained incomplete—the covenant seal of righteousness required in his dispensation. Like Jacob, who could not advance without a change of name, Moses too faced a divine threshold. *(Genesis 17:12-14)*

Circumcision, instituted with Abraham, symbolized the covenant relationship between God and His chosen. It was not the source of righteousness but a *sign* and *seal* of it, as Paul teaches: *"And he received the sign of circumcision, a seal of the righteousness that he had by faith while he was still uncircumcised. So then, he is the father of all who believe but have not been circumcised, in order that righteousness might be credited to them."* (Romans 4:11, NIV)

This outward covenant pointed to an inward reality—a purity of heart and faith that would later be fulfilled in Christ. *"When you came to Christ, you were 'circumcised,' but not by a physical procedure. Christ performed a spiritual circumcision—the cutting away of your sinful nature."* (Colossians 2:11, NLT)

Because Moses had not yet fully aligned with this covenantal requirement of God's chosen people and had not circumcised his son, God confronted him on his journey back to Egypt: *"At a lodging place on the way, the LORD met Moses and was about to kill him. But Zipporah took a flint knife, cut off her son's foreskin and touched Moses' feet with it. 'Surely you are a bridegroom of blood to me,' she said. So He let him alone."* (Exodus 4:24–26, NIV)

In this sobering moment, the principle of divine order was reaffirmed: even those chosen, trained, and called must complete every measure of consecration before advancing. The act of circumcision—performed by Zipporah—secured Moses' covenant standing and symbolically sealed his readiness for the next prerequisite: *Sacrifice.*

This scene underscores a vital truth: **God's call does not override His conditions.** Consecration must be complete—both outwardly and inwardly—before one is entrusted with divine power.

Moses' story reveals that consecration is not only the end of one phase but the threshold of another—a finishing and a beginning. It marks the release from the old and the readiness for the new. Through external stripping and internal purification, Moses emerged as a vessel fit for divine use, ready to embody the righteousness and faith necessary to bear the weight of God's covenant work.

The wilderness had done its work. The prince had died. The deliverer had been born.

CONSECRATION ON A CORPORATE SCALE – The Case of Achan and Israel

JOSHUA AND THE ISRAELITES: The Danger of Hidden Sin

To break from individual pattern bearers and expand our view, consider a powerful corporate example of the Principle of Consecration in *Joshua chapter 7*. After their triumphant conquest of Jericho, the Israelites were poised to swiftly take the land of Ai. Yet, defeat came unexpectedly.

Achan, one of the Israelites, sinned by secretly keeping some of the devoted things—precious spoils the LORD had commanded to be destroyed—as a personal treasure. *"When I saw among the spoils a beautiful Babylonian garment, two hundred shekels of silver, and a wedge of gold weighing fifty shekels, I coveted them and took them. And there they are, hidden in the earth in the midst of my tent, with the silver under it."* (Joshua 7:21, NKJV)

This breach of consecration brought God's anger upon the entire nation, leading to their defeat and the death of thirty-six soldiers. Distraught, Joshua sought God's guidance, who revealed the sin in Israel's camp and instructed Joshua to have the people consecrate themselves. God said through Joshua:

"Get up, sanctify the people, and say, 'Sanctify yourselves for tomorrow, because thus says the LORD God of Israel: There is an accursed thing in your midst, O Israel; you cannot stand before your enemies until you take away the accursed thing from among you.'" (Joshua 7:13, NKJV)

The Timeless Principle of Purging Sin

This story teaches that until the 'accursed thing'—the sin or impurity—is removed, God's people cannot stand victoriously. The call to consecration is a call to holiness and purity, essential for divine favor and success.

This principle transcends time and applies equally to us today. Without removing sin and the sinful nature's influence, we cannot truly please God or fulfill His purposes.

The apostle Paul articulates this clearly: *"For the sinful nature is always hostile to God. It never did obey God's laws, and it never will. That's why those who are still under the control of their sinful nature can never please God."* (Romans 8:7–8, NLT)

A Corporate Model of Consecration

Achan's sin shows how one person's failure in consecration can hinder an entire community's mission. Likewise, our personal consecration affects those around us and the larger purposes God intends to fulfill through us.

Just as the Israelites had to purify their camp corporately, we too must continually prune and sanctify our lives personally and corporately to move forward in God's plan.

This episode powerfully supports the patterns we observe in individual lives, revealing the Principle of Consecration on a larger scale, reminding us of the gravity of holiness as the foundation for becoming.

DAVID: Consecration in Isolation and Preparation

David's story opens in *1 Samuel 16* with a vivid illustration of the three prerequisites of the Principle of Becoming introduced simultaneously—a prelude to the pattern we observe in all these lives.

God sent the prophet Samuel to anoint Israel's next king, replacing the rebellious Saul. Samuel's instructions and approach reflected consecration's foundational role: *"Consecrate yourselves and come to the sacrifice with me."* (1 Samuel 16:5, NIV)

When all of Jesse's sons presented themselves, none fit God's choice. Only when Samuel called for the youngest, David—tending sheep away from the crowd—did God's Spirit descend powerfully upon him. Then *"Samuel said, 'Send for him; we will not sit down until he arrives.' So he sent for him and had him brought in... Then the Lord said, 'Rise and anoint him; this is the one.' So Samuel took the horn of oil and anointed him in the presence of his brothers, and from that day on the Spirit of the Lord came powerfully upon David."* (1 Samuel 16:11–13, NIV)

Set Apart as the Shepherd Boy

David was the outcast, overlooked by brothers and man alike, yet God's choice was grounded in deeper wisdom: *"The Lord sees not as man sees: man looks on the outward appearance, but the LORD looks on the heart."* (1 Samuel 16:7, ESV)

The prophet Samuel, by anointing David, acted as an instrument of divine transfer to David, sending him well on his way on the path to destiny. In this season of isolation, David faced lions and bears protecting his sheep, gaining courage and faith. His battles with wild beasts symbolized a primal consecration—a refining process developing him for greater spiritual and leadership challenges.

Developing Competency and Character

David's time apart built him into not only a courageous warrior but also a skilled musician, anointing him with gifts later used to console King Saul. This interaction was an early example of *Instruments of Divine Transfer*, with Saul unknowingly preparing the path for David's destiny.

His victory over Goliath was a defining culmination of his primal con-secration—a test proving his readiness to transition into the next phase: the *sacrifice prerequisite*. This battle showcased David's faith in God, a faith forged through his wilderness experiences, setting him fundamentally apart from the fearful Israelite army. *"David said to the Philistine, 'You come against me with sword and spear and javelin, but I come against you in the name of the LORD Almighty... This day the LORD will deliver you into my hands.'"* (1 Samuel 17:45–46, NIV)

From Consecration to Sacrifice

David's story encapsulates the principle that consecration is not simply separation but active preparation—building competency, character, and faith in God's promises. It is this readiness that allows transition to the demanding call of sacrifice and covenant.

King Saul's jealousy and opposition would later become the instruments that propelled David further into his destiny, highlighting again how God uses diverse people and circumstances to move us through every stage of our journey to becoming.

David's early life is a powerful reminder that God sets us apart in seasons of solitude and preparation to build a foundation strong enough to carry us forward into His greater purposes.

DANIEL, SHADRACH, MESHACH, AND ABEDNEGO – Faithful Stewards in Exile

Primal Consecration in Babylon: Standing Firm in Spiritual Integrity

Daniel, Shadrach, Meshach, and Abednego—young men of noble descent—were taken captive to Babylon during the exile foretold by Jeremiah as a consequence of Israel's unfaithfulness to God. This exile was no accident but part of God's sovereign orchestration—divinely manipulated circumstances serving as *Instruments of Divine Transfer*, ushering these four into their season of **Primal Consecration**, the first prerequisite in the journey to become.

King Nebuchadnezzar commanded that young men from Judah's royal families be brought to his palace to be trained in Babylonian ways and prepared for government service: *"Select only strong, healthy, and good-looking young men,"* he said. *"Make sure they are well versed in every branch of learning, are gifted with knowledge and good judgment, and are suited to serve in the royal palace. Train these young men in the language and literature of Babylon."* (Daniel 1:4, NLT)

Daniel and his friends were renamed—Belteshazzar, Shadrach, Meshach, and Abednego—symbols of their Babylonian assimilation. Yet, they stood firm on God's commands.

Refusing the King's Food: A Test of Consecration

Despite the king's provision of rich food and wine, Daniel and his friends refused to defile themselves by partaking in the royal banquet. They recognized that eating the king's food could compromise their covenantal identity, breaking consecration with Yahweh—especially since the Babylonian diet likely violated Mosaic dietary laws and risked association with idol worship (*Leviticus 11*).

Instead, Daniel proposed a test of a simple diet for ten days—water and vegetables. Their overseer agreed, and after the trial, they appeared healthier and better nourished than those who ate the king's food. *"At the end of the ten days Daniel and his three friends looked healthier and better nourished than the young men who had been eating the food assigned by the king. So after that, the attendant fed them only vegetables instead of the food and wine provided for the others."* (Daniel 1:15–16, NLT)

Spiritual Integrity and God's Blessing

Their refusal to compromise was not merely about food but about preserving spiritual integrity and faithfulness to God amidst pressure to conform. As a result, God granted them wisdom and favor, with Daniel receiving the special gift of interpreting visions and dreams.

"God gave these four young men an unusual aptitude for understanding every aspect of literature and wisdom. And God gave Daniel the special ability to interpret the meanings of visions and dreams." (Daniel 1:17, NLT)

The Continuing Lesson: Avoiding Spiritual Compromise

This story speaks a timeless truth: consecration requires ongoing vigilance to avoid even subtle forms of spiritual compromise. The apostle Paul warns believers to discern their actions carefully:

"What am I trying to say? Am I saying that food offered to idols has some significance, or that idols are real gods? No, not at all. I am saying that these sacrifices are offered to demons, not to God. And I don't want you to participate with demons." (1 Corinthians 10:19–20, NLT)

Primal Consecration: Foundation for Destiny

Daniel and his friends' faithfulness in consecration prepared them to receive God's primary deposits—the spiritual gifts and favor necessary to fulfill their divine destiny. This season in Babylon formed the bedrock for their future roles as *Instruments of God* through subsequent prerequisites in their journey to becoming.

Steadfast consecration amid worldly pressures establishes a firm foundation upon which God builds His purposes. When their period of preparation was complete and they were presented before the king, the Scripture records: *"Whenever the king consulted them in any matter requiring wisdom and balanced judgment, he found them ten times more capable than any of the magicians and enchanters in his entire kingdom."* (Daniel 1:20, NLT)

Because they remained faithful to their consecration to the one true God, they were elevated above all others, set apart in wisdom, favor, and divine promotion.

ESTHER – Primal Consecration Through Preparation and Divine Favor

Divinely Positioned for Purpose

During the third year of King Xerxes' rule over the vast Medo-Persian Empire—spanning from India to Ethiopia—the realm witnessed grandeur and opulence, represented by a prolonged series of banquets.

These banquets lasted a full 180 days and were followed by a banquet for all the people, from the greatest to the least, who were present in the fortress of Susa. (Esther 1:1–9)

These royal festivities formed the backdrop for a divine orchestration that would initiate the journey of one of Scripture's profound Pattern Bearers: **Esther**.

After Queen Vashti's defiance and subsequent banishment—a pivotal event ordained by God's sovereign hand—the royal court sought a new queen to fill the vacant throne. Xerxes issued a decree to gather the most beautiful young women from across the empire to be presented before him. Among them was Esther, a young Jewish woman residing in Susa, the empire's seat of power.

The Season of Primal Consecration

Esther's inclusion marked the commencement of her **Primal Consecration** phase—the first prerequisite in the journey to become. The young women underwent a meticulous, year-long process of transformation: *"Before a young woman's turn came to go in to King Xerxes, she had to complete twelve months of beauty treatments prescribed for the women, six months with oil of myrrh and six with perfumes and cosmetics."* (Esther 2:12, NIV)

Symbolically, this period was far more than physical beautification—it was divine preparation. God was setting Esther apart, refining and enhancing her for the purpose she was called to fulfill. This twelve-month consecration represented a season of waiting, transformation, and alignment with God's greater plan—equipping her for the challenges and elevation to come.

The Instrument of Divine Transfer: Hegai the Eunuch

Integral to Esther's rise was her favor with Hegai, the king's eunuch and custodian of the harem. This divinely orchestrated relationship became an *Instrument of Divine Transfer*, positioning Esther advantageously within the palace.

"Esther also was taken to the king's palace and entrusted to Hegai, who had charge of the harem. She pleased him and won his favor. Immediately he provided her with her beauty treatments and special food. He assigned to her seven female attendants selected from the king's palace and moved her and her attendants into the best place in the harem." (Esther 2:8–9, NIV)

This illustrates how, in our own journey, God appoints people and orchestrates circumstances to move us forward at the right time. Whether friend or stranger, these instruments function impartially yet purposefully to bring about His will.

Position Is Not the End, But a Transition

It is crucial to understand that Esther's elevation to queen—though significant—was not the culmination of her journey. As with all Pattern Bearers, **position alone does not equal fulfillment of destiny**. Becoming queen was a transition, a passage into the next prerequisite: *Sacrifice.*

The real purpose of Esther's position was yet to be revealed, as she would soon be called to risk her life to intercede for her people. Thus, position in God's plan is never for prestige but for purpose.

This warns us never to grow lax or boastful in any station of power we hold. To God, such positions are tools—temporary thrones of preparation facilitating our progression toward the fullness of what He has ordained us to become, not status symbols or final destinations.

Esther's story powerfully exemplifies faithful consecration, divine favor, and humble readiness—the understanding that every promotion is preparation, and every stage of favor is a call to deeper surrender in the journey of becoming.

TRANSITIONING SEASONS: FROM CONSECRATION TO SACRIFICE

God's perspective transcends the personal—He sees beyond individual lives to generations and nations. When He speaks to you, His word carries authority not only for you but for those who come after. You are a conduit, an ambassador representing Him to the world (Isaiah 43:10–12).

This divine assignment ensures that life and grace accompany every mission. Fear has no place: *"The LORD is my light and my salvation—whom shall I fear? The LORD is the strength of my life—of whom shall I be afraid?"* (Psalm 27:1, NKJV)

Understanding when to move into the next prerequisite requires discernment of your season. *"To everything there is a season, a time for every purpose under heaven."* (Ecclesiastes 3:1, NKJV) Your divine assignment is appointed for such a time—you are not just relevant but necessary. Some blessings and lessons only unfold when you enter the right timing. *"He has made everything beautiful in its time."* (Ecclesiastes 3:11, NKJV)

We live now in the dispensation of the Holy Spirit. *"The sons of Issachar... had understanding of the times, to know what Israel ought to do."* (1 Chronicles 12:32, NKJV)

And Jesus promised, *"When He, the Spirit of truth, has come, He will guide you into all truth."* (John 16:13, NKJV). Through Him, we discern our seasons with clarity.

Therefore, hear the call for consecration and heed to it: *"Get out! Get out and leave your captivity, where everything you touch is unclean. Get out of there and purify yourselves, you who carry home the sacred objects of the LORD.* "(Isaiah 52:11, NLT)

Training Through Trials: Qualification for Divine Purpose

God often uses testing circumstances to prepare you—emotionally, spiritually, and physically. Difficult times test endurance and faithfulness, qualifying you to carry heavier burdens. Stress reveals whether you will break or stand firm. In these moments, ask yourself:

- Could God be training me for something greater?

- Is He searching for a strong-willed person to do a difficult work?

Be still and trust in His sovereignty: *"Be still, and know that I am God."* (Psalm 46:10, NKJV)Like Daniel and his friends, God invests spiritual gifts, wisdom, and new capacities during these primal consecration seasons: *"God gave them knowledge and skill in all literature and wisdom; and Daniel had understanding in all visions and dreams."* (Daniel 1:17, NKJV)

Through this, you gain new understanding of your identity in Christ and your divine purpose.

Avoiding the Pitfall of Misplaced Priorities

Like Solomon's pursuit of meaning, many chase wealth or power without finding true fulfillment: *"Fear God and keep His commandments, for this is the whole duty of man."* (Ecclesiastes 12:13, NIV)

True fulfillment requires intentional completion of your primal consecration. Skipping foundational preparation leads to correction or stagnation—a bitter, unfulfilled life. God may chasten you as He did Jacob and

Moses, or you may linger in wasted potential. The purpose of this book is to illuminate your current place so you can recalibrate before it's too late.

The Deadline of Consecration: A Set Time

Every pattern bearer's journey shows that consecration is a season with a divinely appointed deadline. Esther's twelve months of preparation *(Esther 2:12)*, Jacob's fourteen years of service to Laban *(Genesis 29–31)*, Daniel and his friends' three-year training *(Daniel 1:5)*, and Moses' forty years in the wilderness—each represents a unique but appointed season of divine preparation.

The first two prerequisites—**Consecration** and **Sacrifice**—carry set time-lines, individually tailored by God. These seasons prepare you for the third and final prerequisite: **Anointing**, the place of divine appointment and fullness.

Facing Your Goliath: The Test of Transition

Every David faces a Goliath before advancing to the place of authority. This Goliath may appear as daunting projects, impossible dreams, or fierce opposition. No one else can fight this battle for you. Discipleship demands personal confrontation with your giant.

Consider:

- For Moses, it was facing a past he wished to forget.

- For Joseph, serving faithfully as a slave despite princely destiny.

- For Abraham, leaving the familiar to pursue the impossible.

- For Daniel, Shadrach, Meshach, and Abednego, defying decrees to uphold their faith.

Faithfulness and discernment of God's will mark readiness to conquer. When Goliath falls, favor and authority follow—doors open, resistance breaks, and you walk in divine power. *"So David prevailed over the Philistine with a sling and a stone."* (1 Samuel 17:50, NKJV)

Your Season of Becoming

Recognize your window of transition. Will you step forward in faith or shrink back? *"Not by might nor by power, but by My Spirit," says the LORD of hosts.* (Zechariah 4:6, NKJV)

This is your moment to move—trusting the deliberate hand of God to carry you from consecration into sacrifice, and onward toward the anointing that crowns your becoming.

PREREQUISITE TWO: SACRIFICE

Introduction: The Threshold of Sacrifice

After the work of consecration, the next essential step in your journey to become is **sacrifice**. This stage is more than a requirement—it is a furnace that tests every part of your allegiance to God.

As Scripture consistently reveals, **no sacrifice is accepted except by fire**. The fire represents both the *testing* and the *approval* of God—it purifies intention, proves loyalty, and ensures your offering is truly worthy in His eyes (Leviticus 9:24; Hebrews 12:29).

In this prerequisite, boundaries are drawn around our liberties, and self-will yields to God's sovereign hand. God will never entrust great things to those He cannot restrain. Here, the heart learns surrender, discipline, and the posture of mature stewardship.

Sacrifice is where loyalty is tested, sources are exposed, and everything that contends with God for your affection comes into the light. If your trust or your treasure rests on anything but Him, this is where the altar will demand it.

Surrender, Refinement, and the Furnace of Testing

Sacrifice is a deeply personal process—*tailored for each person.* As we will see through the lives of our Pattern Bearers—both those already introduced and those yet to come—no two journeys are identical, yet the principle remains the same.

This is the place where your ability to lay down *everything* is tested by God Himself. The idols of the heart, those things too precious to release, must be placed upon the altar. Whether it be reputation, comfort, relationships, ambition, resources, or dreams, nothing remains untested.

As Christ Himself said, *"For where your treasure is, there your heart will be also."* (Matthew 6:21, NIV)

This season exposes the truest desires of the heart. Only when the deepest longing of your soul is God Himself are you ready for covenantal partnership with Him.

It is in the place of sacrifice that genuine, *enduring covenants* are forged between man and God—covenants that heaven recognizes and honors.

When Surrender Unlocks the Next Level

For some, the season of sacrifice feels like *pain, loss, or trial*; for others, it is marked by a deep internal struggle—the dying to self that opens the door to resurrection life.

The sooner we yield, the sooner transformation occurs; the quicker we bring the entirety of our hearts and lives as living sacrifices (Romans 12:1), the faster the season passes.

Surrender is the golden key—a heart posture that cannot be faked. It is not merely the laying down of actions but the yielding of desire itself. When true surrender is reached—the sacrifice is complete, maturity is proven, and transition to the next stage becomes inevitable.

The LORD Himself declared: *"Whoever wants to be My disciple must deny themselves and take up their cross daily and follow Me."* (Luke 9:23, NIV)

Sacrifice is the place where self-interest dies and divine purpose is born. It is the crucible where heaven witnesses maturity—proof that you are ready to bear greater spiritual authority and anointing.

The stories ahead will unveil sacrifice in its true form—what it costs, what it produces, and how it propels you closer to the *fullness of what God has called you to become.*

ABRAM: The Journey of Faith, Covenant, and Transformation

From Abram to Father of Many Nations

In responding to God's call in Genesis 12, Abram embarked upon his first prerequisite in the journey to become—*Primal Consecration.* This journey required him to leave behind all he knew: his father's household, his people, and his nation. That separation embodied the essence of consecration—being set apart for divine purpose.

He fulfilled this act of faith when he arrived in the land God showed him, Canaan, thus completing his consecration season and entering the second prerequisite—the season of sacrifice (Genesis 12:7).

Upon arrival, the LORD appeared to Abram and promised: *"To your descendants I will give this land."* (Genesis 12:7, NKJV)

This moment confirmed Abram's obedience and marked a divine invitation to build his altar—to dedicate himself to God's will—the closing act of consecration and the opening gate of sacrifice.

Testing, Warfare, and Divine Partnership

Abram's season of sacrifice was marked by testing and warfare that shaped and proved his faith. When famine struck, driving him to Egypt, and when conflicts arose between his herdsmen and Lot's, Abram's choices reflected restraint, trust, and divine reliance. Later, when Lot was taken captive, Abram mobilized 318 trained men and pursued the invaders, recovering all that was lost.

After his victory over the allied kings, Abram encountered Melchizedek, king of Salem and priest of the Most High God. Melchizedek brought forth bread and wine, blessing him with these words:

"Blessed be Abram by God Most High, Creator of heaven and earth. And blessed be God Most High, who has delivered your enemies into your hand." (Genesis 14:19–20, NIV)

In reverence, Abram gave Melchizedek a tenth of all he recovered—a gesture of honor and recognition of divine provision. Melchizedek thus became an Instrument of Divine Transfer, blessing Abram and equipping him for the next stage of his journey. This encounter marked divine approval and advancement within the furnace of sacrifice.

Covenant and Faith: The Hallmarks of Sacrifice

It is within the sacrifice prerequisite that God begins to establish *covenant* with man—signifying maturity, intentionality, and spiritual responsibility.

In Genesis 15, amidst Abram's concern over childlessness, he said: *"Sovereign LORD, what can you give me since I remain childless...?"* (Genesis 15:2, NIV)

God responded by promising a son from his own body and a lineage as countless as the stars. *"Look up at the sky and count the stars—if indeed you can count them. So shall your offspring be."* (Genesis 15:5, NIV) Abram believed the LORD, *"and He credited it to him as righteousness."* (Genesis 15:6, NIV)

Faith became the engine propelling Abram forward through sacrifice—pleasing the LORD and securing covenant relationship. God instructed him to prepare a sacrifice and declared His promise: *"To your descendants I give this land, from the river of Egypt to the great river, the Euphrates."* (Genesis 15:18, NIV)

Grace Amid Human Frailty

Even amid human error, grace sustains those in the season of sacrifice. Though Abram faltered by accepting Hagar and fathering Ishmael (Genesis 16), God reaffirmed His covenant.

When Abram was ninety-nine, the Lord appeared to him and said: *"I am God Almighty; walk before Me faithfully and be blameless."* (Genesis 17:1, NIV)

In that encounter, God renamed Abram to **Abraham**, meaning *"father of many nations,"* and Sarai to **Sarah**, meaning *"princess."* *"No longer will you be called Abram; your name will be Abraham, for I have made you a father of many nations."* (Genesis 17:5, NIV) *"As for Sarai your wife, you are no longer to call her Sarai; her name will be Sarah."* (Genesis 17:15, NIV)

These renamings signified elevation through transformation—Abraham's identity now reflected his divine destiny, and Sarah's her noble purpose. This was not mere name change but covenantal redefinition—where divine purpose overtakes human potential.

The Fulfillment and the Ultimate Test

God's promise was fulfilled with the birth of Isaac, the child of promise, to Abraham and Sarah in their old age (Genesis 21:1–3). The covenant was sealed through obedience, for *"Abraham circumcised his son Isaac when he was eight days old, as God commanded him."* (Genesis 21:4, NKJV)

But the pinnacle of sacrifice came when God tested Abraham, saying: *"Take your son, your only son Isaac, whom you love and... sacrifice him there as a burnt offering."* (Genesis 22:2, NIV)

No sacrifice is accepted without fire (Leviticus 1:9), and this command became the furnace that refined Abraham's heart. Isaac was never meant to die—the true sacrifice was Abraham's will. When Abraham obeyed, the LORD intervened: *"Do not lay a hand on the boy... Now I know that you fear God, because you have not withheld from Me your son, your only son.*" (Genesis 22:12, NIV)

God then swore by Himself, sealing His covenant with irrevocable promise: "*I swear by Myself, declares the LORD, that because you have done this… I will surely bless you and make your descendants as numerous as the stars in the sky… and through your offspring all nations on earth will be blessed.*" (Genesis 22:16–18, NIV)

This was the apex of Abraham's journey—the altar of ultimate surrender and the threshold into destiny fullness.

Sacrifice: The Place of Covenant, Maturity, and Transformation

Sacrifice is the sacred ground where covenant is cut, maturity is proven, and transformation takes root. Here, God engages His servants in deep communion through surrender and obedience.

In this place, identities are refined, purpose clarified, and destiny forged. Abraham's story reveals that moving through sacrifice requires faith to obey, courage to release, and the willingness to lay the cherished upon the altar for God's highest will.

Preparing for Destiny's Fulfillment

From this point forward, Abraham could rest in confidence that God's promises were secure. The foundation had been laid; the covenant established. His next steps led toward the final prerequisite—**Anointing and Divine Appointment**—the manifestation of all that sacrifice had prepared him to receive.

In the next chapter, we will explore how Abraham's journey—and those of other Pattern Bearers—culminates in the fullness of their God-ordained destinies.

JACOB – From Consecration to Sacrifice

After returning to the land God had originally directed him to, Jacob—now called Israel—completed a profound act of reconciliation with his brother Esau. This significant moment set the stage for a new chapter in Jacob's journey. As recorded in Genesis 33:18–20 (NIV):

After Jacob came from Paddan Aram, he arrived safely at the city of Shechem in Canaan and camped within sight of the city. For a hundred pieces of silver, he bought from the sons of Hamor, the father of Shechem, the plot of ground where he pitched his tent. There he set up an altar and called it El Elohe Israel.

By building this altar and calling on the name of Yahweh, Jacob was not merely repeating his grandfather Abraham's pattern—he was enacting the very principle of spiritual sacrifice as the next stage in his journey of becoming. Repetition of this altar-building pattern symbolizes the conscious transition from primal consecration to the prerequisite of sacrifice—a deliberate and intentional forging of covenant with God at a new and higher level.

The Return to Bethel: The Renewal and Cleansing

Jacob's spiritual discernment is revealed again when God prompts him to return to Bethel—the very site of his first revelation in the previous prerequisite. Genesis 35:1 (NIV) records:

Then God said to Jacob, "Go up to Bethel and settle there, and build an altar there to God, who appeared to you when you were fleeing from your brother Esau."

Jacob, understanding the spiritual weight of this moment, instructs his entire household to prepare for sacrifice and renewal:

So Jacob said to his household and to all who were with him, "Get rid of the foreign gods you have with you, and purify yourselves and change your clothes. Then come, let us go up to Bethel, where I will build an altar to God, who answered me in the day of my distress and who has been with me wherever I have gone." (Genesis 35:2–3, NIV)

This profound moment teaches that as we transition into deeper and higher places with God, we must shed all idols, purify our lives, and set ourselves intentionally apart for Him. The sacrifice prerequisite entails this continual cleansing and increased intentionality. Jacob's altar in Bethel—El-Bethel, meaning "God of Bethel"—established an even more defined relationship with God, reflecting a higher level of covenant and commitment.

Life's Journey, God's Guidance

Jacob's story teaches us that the journey to become is not a side project; it is woven into the very fabric of daily life, with all its joys, sorrows, responsibilities, and challenges. The sacrifice prerequisite extends through life's seasons—even grief and loss. As Jacob journeyed from Bethel toward Ephrath, his beloved wife Rachel died during the birth of Benjamin—a painful trial.

He grieved, yet pressed on, ultimately reuniting with his aged father Isaac, who passed away at 180 years. Despite sorrow and transitions, Jacob remained planted in the land of promise, leading his family and pressing forward in faith.

The Ongoing Fire of Sacrifice

Even during periods of seeming stability and blessing, the sacrifice prerequisite continues. Although Jacob had settled in Canaan for a time, his journey was far from complete. God's design was for his formation to continue through challenges intertwined with the lives of his sons, especially Joseph. As we will soon see, God's process of refinement was not finished—the ultimate test, the fire that would further purify Jacob for fullness of purpose, was still ahead.

The Sacrifice Prerequisite: Patterns of Covenant and Maturity

Jacob's narrative reveals that in the second prerequisite:

- God often renews and expands covenants made in earlier seasons (Genesis 35:9–13).

- Our intentional actions—cleansing, sacrifice, altar-building—signal our readiness for deeper relationship.

- The journey incorporates every facet of life, requiring resilience, humility, and ongoing faith, no matter what comes.

Jacob's story reminds us not to see tests or hardships as interruptions, but as integral to the process of becoming. The fires of sacrifice prepare us for true appointment—just as Jacob's was to be intertwined with the destiny of his son Joseph and the future of the entire nation.

As we pause here, know that the final fires of qualification lie ahead for Jacob, marking his transition into the ultimate prerequisite, where true destiny, anointing, and legacy await. We'll explore this final transition in the next chapter.

JOSEPH – The Season of Sacrifice and Faithful Stewardship

After being set apart from his father's household by God's sovereign hand—who used his brothers as instruments of divine transfer to launch him into the first prerequisite of the journey to become, primal consecration—Joseph was now ready to transition into the second prerequisite: sacrifice.

Joseph was purchased by Potiphar, a new channel of divine transfer. Potiphar's house represented the gateway from the season of consecration into the season of sacrifice. Here, Joseph faced the crucial test: had he truly put to death the negative deeds of the flesh? Would he resist the selfish desires that corrupt leaders and ultimately destroy both themselves and those they govern?

Potiphar entrusted Joseph with everything—his household, his property, and his affairs. Joseph's integrity and stewardship gained him favor; he was concerned only with performing his duty well. Potiphar, therefore, concerned himself only with what he would eat. Because of Joseph, he had no cares with the menial tasks of managing his household when greater responsibilities demanded his attention. Potiphar's trust reflected Joseph's faithful management *(Genesis 39:4–6)*.

The Test of Flesh and Faithfulness

The sacrifice prerequisite is not merely about external service but about internal governance—mastery over the self. Joseph's ultimate test came through Potiphar's wife. Her repeated advances were not just temptation but a divine instrument of transfer, probing whether Joseph's heart prioritized loyalty to God and good governance over selfish lust and immorality.

Succumbing to evil sexual temptation reveals a leader's selfish character, foreshadowing future ruinous governance where personal gratification replaces responsibility to others. Joseph, however, stood firm:

"How then could I do such a wicked thing and sin against God?" (Genesis 39:9, NIV)

This response revealed his heart's alignment and readiness for higher responsibility.

Accused and Imprisoned: Progressing through Trials

Though innocent, Joseph's rejection of temptation led to false accusations by Potiphar's wife. Consequently, Potiphar transferred Joseph to prison—a place still within the boundaries of sacrifice but one that further tested and refined him (Genesis 39:20–23).

In prison, Joseph's faithfulness did not waver. His admirable stewardship promoted him to oversee all prisoners, a position of responsibility and trust (Genesis 39:22–23). God's presence was evident despite harsh conditions—preparing Joseph for his destiny.

Divine Gifts and the Interpretation of Dreams

God's equipping of Joseph became evident when Pharaoh's chief cupbearer and baker were troubled by dreams during incarceration. Joseph interpreted their dreams with divine insight (Genesis 40), accurately predicting the fate of both men.

Before the cupbearer's restoration, Joseph wisely requested: *"When all goes well with you, please remember me and show me kindness; mention me to Pharaoh and get me out of this prison."* (Genesis 40:14, NIV)

This plea reflected his understanding that God's timing was yet to be fulfilled.

The Delay and Divine Timing

Despite Joseph's faithful service and prophetic gift, the cupbearer forgot him after being restored—an example of divine delay and testing of endurance. Joseph remained in prison an additional two years (Genesis 41:1).

This period aligns with the principle that every stage in the journey to become has its set time; it will neither finish early nor late but unfold according to divine ordination.

The Divine Appointment and Rise to Power

Finally, Pharaoh experienced troubling dreams God used to orchestrate Joseph's release. By divine design, the cupbearer remembered Joseph at the appointed time, and Joseph was summoned before Pharaoh (Genesis 41:14–16).

Joseph's wisdom impressed Pharaoh. With God's gifting fully matured, Joseph interpreted Pharaoh's dreams accurately and offered strategic counsel to prepare for famine.

Pharaoh exalted Joseph to second-in-command over all Egypt, a world power of his day (Genesis 41:39–41). Joseph had arrived at the final prerequisite—anointing leading to divine appointment. He embodied prudence, governance, and faithfulness, having maximized every opportunity and trial.

Joseph's Legacy: Faithfulness in Position

Joseph's journey teaches that power and position are not mere privileges but tools of stewardship granted for greater purposes. Potiphar, the prison warden, and Pharaoh each entrusted him fully, impressed by his integrity and wisdom.

Despite being the youngest and betrayed by brothers, Joseph's faith remained steadfast. His gifts—spiritual and practical—were purposefully honed through divine seasons of testing and growth.

He stood prepared, a prudent steward ready for God's ultimate plan: preserving lives through famine and advancing God's covenant promises to Abraham.

A Final Reflection

Joseph's story is a testament that those who journey to become seize divine opportunity by walking faithfully in every season—primal consecration, sacrifice, and anointing. His rise was no accident but a divine unfolding built on integrity, patience, and submission.

In the coming chapter, we will see how Joseph's advancement played a pivotal role in the unfolding destiny of his father Jacob, interweaving the pattern bearers' journeys in God's grand design.

MOSES – Sacrifice, Surrender, and Emergence

Moses emerged from his season of primal consecration a changed man—stripped of pride, self-reliance, and worldly strength. All the confidence he once possessed, the courage to confront injustice (seen when he slew the Egyptian who oppressed a fellow Jew), was burned away by the fires of exile and humility.

By the time God spoke and called him to return to Egypt, Moses saw himself as insufficient—fearful of Pharaoh and haunted by the past he longed to escape.

"Who am I that I should go to Pharaoh and bring the Israelites out of Egypt?" (Exodus 3:11, NIV), Moses asked, doubting his worth and ability. Even when God assured him of divine company and empowerment, Moses hesitated, insisting:

"What if they do not believe me?" (Exodus 4:1, NIV).

"I am slow of speech and tongue." (Exodus 4:10, NIV)

God, unwilling to call another, met Moses' weaknesses with provision—his brother Aaron as helper and spokesman. Moses accepted, humbling himself, submitting all pride, comfort, excuses, and self-despising to God's process; thus began his sacrifice prerequisite.

The Fire of Sacrifice: Surrender and Transformation

Moses had to sacrifice his timidity and self-doubt, embrace courage he did not feel, and obey God's call against every instinct to flee and hide. The sacrifice prerequisite demanded utter surrender—relinquishing self-protective tendencies, comfort zones, and the need for self-assurance in favor of faith and obedience.

Returning to Egypt, Moses confronted not only his fears but a stubborn Pharaoh who resisted and increased the burdens of Israel. He even faced and complaint from his own people:

They said to Moses, *"May the LORD look on you and judge you! You have made us obnoxious to Pharaoh and his officials and have put a sword in their hand to kill us.'"* (Exodus 5:21, NIV)

Leading a grumbling, fearful people tested Moses' humility and patience, tempering him through repeated opposition. Each encounter with Pharaoh, each plague that fell, was God's crucible transforming Moses. Once hesitant, Moses grew into his authority, communicating intimately with God, strengthening in courage and resolve.

Sacrifice Prepares for Anointing

The sacrifice prerequisite for Moses reached its climax with the tenth plague—the death of Egypt's firstborn, the institution of Passover, and the final deliverance. Pharaoh, undone by grief and loss, finally relented, sending Moses and Israel out of Egypt (Exodus 12:31).

As the last carriage crossed the gates, Moses' season of sacrifice reached its end. From shepherd in exile to leader of a nation, Moses was now ready for the final prerequisite—the anointing that establishes divine appointment. The journey had qualified him: God could now trust Moses with leadership, knowing His servant had surrendered self for the sake of God and His people.

The Journey's Lesson

Moses' story reveals that God does not anoint the untested or the unwilling. Each stage of the journey to become is designed to strip away hindrances, test motives, and forge the character necessary for true spiritual authority. Until humility, obedience, and endurance are proven, anointing waits—as does the fullness of purpose.

In the chapter to come, we'll continue Moses' journey through the lens of divine appointment—the place where all preparation, sacrifice, and surrender find their ultimate fulfillment in God's plan.

THE DIVINE BLUEPRINT OF THE PRINCIPLE OF BECOMING:

A Symbolic Revelation

THE TABERNACLE:

A Divine Metaphor for The Journey of Becoming

The Tabernacle, as outlined in the Scriptures—specifically in Exodus 25–27 and 30—serves as a profound symbol of the process of spiritual transformation and the progressive steps in the Principle of Becoming. Its intricate design reflects a divine architecture that maps the journey of every believer, emphasizing that reaching the highest levels of intimacy and service with God requires preparation, purity, and authority beyond mere participation.

This sacred structure was divided into three main compartments: the outer court, the inner court, and the Holy of Holies—the very innermost chamber where the presence of God dwelled. To even enter the outer court, one had to be a consecrated priest—a vessel set apart, cleansed, and qualified to approach God. The outer court symbolized primal consecration—the foundational step in the journey to become, where dedication and sanctification are first enacted.

Outer Court: The Baseline of Consecration

The outer court represented the initial level of intimacy, where sacrifices were offered and daily duties—such as maintaining the altar—were performed. Only priests, who were consecrated, could access this space—a place epitomizing the outward act of dedication necessary to begin the journey.

The importance of this stage is underscored by the fact that even the high priest was required to be consecrated before entering the innermost of God's presence. Without this, no one could qualify to stand in the gap for their generation.

This level symbolizes the first prerequisite—primal consecration—the act of setting oneself apart for God's divine purpose. If we fail here, the pathway to higher realms remains closed, and our efforts are reduced to mere religion rather than authentic service.

Inner Court: A Higher Calling

Beyond the outer court was the inner court, where more intentional and sacred duties were performed—such as the lighting of the Menorah and the presentation of incense upon the altar of incense. Entry into this space signified a deeper level of qualification, requiring greater intention, purity, and focus.

This two-level separation underscores the second prerequisite—sacrifice—a higher level of commitment that demands ongoing dedication, humility, and purity.

The inner court represented a higher level of stewardship—an increased capacity for leadership and service—where trustworthiness and spiritual discipline determine access. It was a stepping stone, symbolizing a matured heart and a more intentional life dedicated to stewarding divine responsibilities.

The Holy of Holies: The Final Threshold

The innermost chamber, the Holy of Holies, was where God's presence dwelled, accessible only once a year by the high priest through a sacred, costly act of sacrifice—upon the altar of incense and through the blood of atonement. No one could enter unworthily; access was allowed only after full cleansing and sanctification, symbolizing the final prerequisite—the place of divine appointment and full maturity.

This sacred space underscores that only those fully consecrated, purified, and prepared can stand in the highest realm of divine intimacy—where the final act of sacrifice and covenant occur. Without meeting the stringent requirements of holiness and obedience, no one could qualify for such divine fellowship, and the nation's destiny could perish.

The New Covenant: A Bold Approach

Today, through Christ Jesus, believers no longer need to wait once a year or rely on earthly priests to stand in the gap. Hebrews 10:19–22 (NIV) affirms:

"Therefore, brothers and sisters, since we have confidence to enter the Most Holy Place by the blood of Jesus, by a new and living way opened for us through the curtain, that is, his body, and since we have a great priest over the house of God, let us draw near to God with a sincere heart in full assurance of faith."

This truth empowers us in the Principle of Becoming: we can approach the throne of grace with boldness—but only after we have fully aligned ourselves with the process, meeting the divine standards of consecration, sacrifice, and maturity.

The Call to Stewardship and Authority

The divine protocol in the Tabernacle teaches us that God entrusts higher levels of authority—kingship and priesthood—only to those who have proven their readiness through sacrifice. The journey from humility to divine appointment is built on continuous surrender, purity, and faithful stewardship.

In God's economy, many are called, but only the faithful—those who have walked through the stages of consecration and sacrifice—reach the final realm of divine appointment, where they wield authority as stewards of God's kingdom purposes; only these are chosen.

Closing Thought

The divine blueprint of the Tabernacle vividly illustrates that the Principle of Becoming is designed to nurture generations of men and women who are fully prepared—consecrated, sacrificed, and mature—ready to fulfill their divine destinies and carry the authority of heaven.

It emphasizes that the higher you ascend, the greater the sacrifice, and the more vital it is to remain faithful in every season of testing and transformation.

As we prepare to delve into the stories of our Pattern Bearers, let this divine pattern remind us: the journey to the highest realms of divine purpose requires intentionality, sanctification, and unwavering commitment—faithful stewardship is the key to unlocking the fullness of our calling.

DAVID – The Season of Sacrifice and Testing

After David slew Goliath, he was brought before King Saul, holding the Philistine's head as proof of victory. Saul asked, "Tell me about your father, young man." David replied, "His name is Jesse, and we live in Bethlehem" *(1 Samuel 17:55–58)*. From that day forward, Saul kept David with him and would not let him return home. This marked the end of David's season of primal consecration—a time of obscurity and separation unto the LORD—that had prepared him for the trials ahead.

Within that consecration phase, David had received spiritual deposits: gifts, abilities, and self-discovery, sharpening him for greater challenges. When Saul kept him close, David shifted into the second prerequisite of the journey to become—*sacrifice*—with Saul serving as an instrument of divine transfer.

Covenant Brotherhood and Rising Responsibility

David forged a deep covenant bond with Jonathan, Saul's son, becoming covenant brothers. Whatever task Saul assigned, David executed with success. Recognizing his leadership and favor among the people, Saul appointed him commander over the army, further establishing his growing influence (*1 Samuel 18:1–4; 18:5*).

Though David now held position and power, he remained firmly within his sacrifice prerequisite, only beginning to walk through its tests.

Jealousy, Persecution, and Testing

Victory and popularity often usher in opposition and testing. When the Israelite women sang, *"Saul has slain his thousands, and David his tens of thousands"* (*1 Samuel 18:7, NIV*)

Saul's jealousy ignited. Fearing David's rising fame, he began to see him as a threat to the throne (*1 Samuel 18:8–9*). The Spirit of the LORD had departed from Saul, replaced by a tormenting spirit that drove him into madness.

David's role as Saul's harp player—once a ministry of peace—became perilous. Twice, Saul hurled a spear at him, attempting to kill him, but David escaped both times (*1 Samuel 18:10–11*). From that day forward, Saul viewed David with fear and hostility.

Faithfulness Amid Danger

Despite persecution, David remained humble and faithful. Saul sent him on dangerous military campaigns, hoping he would be slain, yet each time David prevailed, increasing his fame and deepening Saul's envy (*1 Samuel*

18:28–30). Assassination attempts followed, but Jonathan's loyal intercession preserved David's life for a time (*1 Samuel 19:1–7*).

Fugitive Days and Growing Influence

Branded a rebel, David fled from Saul's court, becoming a fugitive. During this wilderness season, many outcasts, debtors, and discontented men gathered around him, forming a band of devoted followers (*1 Samuel 22:1–2*). Even while hunted, David's leadership and influence expanded—proof that divine favor is not limited by circumstance.

The Test of Mercy and Righteousness

A defining test came in the wilderness of En-Gedi. Saul entered a cave to relieve himself, unaware that David and his men were hidden deeper inside. Though urged to strike Saul down, David refused, saying, *"The LORD forbid that I should do this thing to my master, the LORD's anointed"* (*1 Samuel 24:1–7*).

Later, in the hills of Hakilah, David again spared Saul's life, taking only his spear and water jug as evidence of his restraint (*1 Samuel 26:1–12*). Both moments revealed the purity of David's heart. In sacrificing pride and vengeance, David preserved his integrity—qualities essential for true kingship.

The Culmination and Transition

After years of testing and endurance, the day of transition came. Saul and his son Jonathan fell in battle (*1 Samuel 31*). Upon hearing the news, David mourned deeply, yet moved forward in obedience. He went up to Judah, and there the men of Judah anointed him king (*2 Samuel 2:1–4*).

This marked the close of David's season of sacrifice and the dawn of his final prerequisite—*Anointing and Divine Appointment*. His journey to kingship had only just begun.

In the following chapter, we will explore how David stepped into the fullness of his divine calling—how his anointing matured into authority, and his appointment into dominion.

DANIEL (WITH SHADRACH, MESHACH, AND ABEDNEGO) – The Fires of Sacrifice and Divine Distinction

When the season of training commanded by King Nebuchadnezzar ended, Daniel and his friends Hananiah, Mishael, and Azariah stood before the king. Scripture records:

"The king talked with them, and he found none equal to Daniel, Hananiah, Mishael, and Azariah; so they entered the king's service. In every matter of wisdom and understanding... he found them ten times better than all the magicians and enchanters in his whole kingdom." (Daniel 1:19–20, NIV)

This moment marked their transition from the season of primal consecration into the rigorous demands of the sacrifice prerequisite. The vessels of divine transfer—Ashpenaz, the chief of staff, and King Nebuchadnezzar himself—served as agents to move them to the next level. Their consecration was validated by a test, as is the established pattern for all pattern bearers; every promotion in God's process is preceded by proving.

Divine Deposits and Testing

Daniel, Shadrach, Meshach, and Abednego received divine deposits during their consecration— *"To these four young men God gave knowledge and understanding of all kinds of literature and learning. And Daniel could understand visions and dreams of all kinds.* "(Daniel 1:17, NIV)

These gifts were not merely for distinction but also for service, opening doors for the next level. Distinct from his friends, Daniel's path was destined to stand uniquely apart.

In Daniel 2, when King Nebuchadnezzar demanded his dream be told and interpreted without revealing it, none of Babylon's wise men could answer—proving the futility of human wisdom and the supremacy of God.

By divine providence, Daniel became the vessel through whom God brought revelation, rescue, and glory. Relying on urgent prayer and the support of his friends, Daniel received the secret in a night vision (Daniel 2:17–19). His response was worship—and the boldness to intercede before the king at the risk of his life.

Arioch, the commander sent to execute the wise men, became the next instrument of divine transfer. Through God's hand, he listened to Daniel, presenting him before the king instead of carrying out his orders. Modern readers must recognize—God will always position people on your path whose choices unlock new levels when you walk in faith and sensitivity to His leading.

Daniel interpreted the king's dream with supernatural accuracy, giving glory to God: *"The great God has shown the king what will take place in the future. The dream is true and its interpretation is trustworthy."* (Daniel 2:45, NIV)

In response, King Nebuchadnezzar declared: *"Surely your God is the God of gods and the Lord of kings and a revealer of mysteries, for you were able to reveal this mystery."* (Daniel 2:47, NIV)

The result: Daniel was elevated to ruler over the province and chief among the wise. By his request—acting as an instrument of divine transfer for his friends—his three companions were also entrusted with high positions (Daniel 2:48–49). Yet promotion was not the end of their process, but rather the proving ground of sacrifice.

The Qualifying Fire: Shadrach, Meshach, and Abednego

For the three friends, a literal crucible awaited in Daniel chapter 3. Their refusal to bow to Nebuchadnezzar's golden statue marked the final test of their sacrifice prerequisite. When threatened with death in the blazing furnace, their response was unwavering:

"Even if He does not [save us], *we want you to know, Your Majesty, that we will not serve your gods."* (Daniel 3:18, NIV)

Their faith demonstrated supreme devotion. God honored them by sending a fourth figure—*"like a son of the gods"*—to walk with them in the flames (Daniel 3:25, NIV). They emerged unharmed, their deliverance broadcasting the supremacy of Yahweh across the world's most powerful empire.

An International Declaration of Reverence

Nebuchadnezzar, deeply moved, issued a royal decree: *"Praise be to the God of Shadrach, Meshach, and Abednego... no other god can save in this way!"* (Daniel 3:28–29, NIV)

Babylon, as the superpower empire ruling over many nations and peoples, broadcast this decree internationally. The king's proclamation called for all peoples, languages, and races within the empire's vast dominion to reverence the Most High God. This moment represents not only divine vindication but a global acknowledgment of Yahweh's supreme power. *(Take note of this, dear reader.)*

Elevated in Authority: The Culmination of Sacrifice

Following their miraculous deliverance, the three were promoted to positions of higher authority in the province of Babylon:

"Then the king promoted Shadrach, Meshach, and Abednego in the province of Babylon." (Daniel 3:30, NIV)

Thus, they ascended into the final prerequisite—the place of anointing and divine appointment. In this highest realm of service and influence, they were empowered to further advance God's purposes openly and effectively. Their journey embodies the truth that true sacrifice yields honor and positions of stewardship, enabling the faithful to execute God's agenda more powerfully.

In the Principle of Becoming, *sacrifice, proven faithfulness, and divine favor combine to elevate God's servants for Kingdom impact. This pattern remains steadfast—a law written by God Himself.*

Daniel's Ongoing Sacrifice and Final Fire

Continuing in the second prerequisite—whether Daniel was absent from the king's court during the fiery furnace ordeal of Shadrach, Meshach, and Abednego, or simply exempt from that trial due to his high favor as a revered dream interpreter and ruler over the province of Babylon—one truth stands: Daniel would not have compromised to worship the golden statue.

In Daniel 4, after interpreting a prophetic dream for Nebuchadnezzar, Daniel boldly counseled the king to repent and show mercy to the poor (Daniel 4:27). The prophecy was fulfilled: Nebuchadnezzar was humbled, living like a wild beast until he acknowledged the supremacy of the Most High God (Daniel 4:32–37).

In the **second international proclamation** to all provinces of his vast empire, Nebuchadnezzar declared: *"How great are his signs, how mighty his wonders! His kingdom is an eternal kingdom; his dominion endures from generation to generation."* (Daniel 4:3, NIV)

This public testimony to Yahweh's power brought God nationwide glory and reverence. Like David, who credited God for his victories, Daniel recognized and praised divine sovereignty, understanding that true progress in the journey to become is inseparable from glorifying God.

Years later, in Daniel 5, the Babylonian empire crumbled under Belshazzar after his blasphemous feast, where temple vessels from Jerusalem were misused for idol worship—a mockery to Yahweh (Daniel 5:24–28). When none could read the mysterious handwriting on the wall, the queen mother—a divinely positioned instrument of transfer—urged Belshazzar to summon Daniel.

Steadfast and content in God, Daniel declined royal rewards but revealed the kingdom's imminent fall. That very night, the Medo-Persian empire replaced Babylon.

In Daniel 6, Darius the Mede appointed Daniel and three others as administrators. Daniel's exceptional spirit soon marked him for rulership over the entire realm (Daniel 6:1–3). Jealous rivals, unable to fault his governance, orchestrated a decree forbidding prayer to any except the king for thirty days. Yet Daniel's unwavering devotion compelled him to pray openly, sealing his fate.

Thrown into the lions' den—a qualifying fire of his sacrifice—Daniel emerged unharmed through divine intervention: an angel closed the lions' mouths (Daniel 6:22). The next day, King Darius joyfully proclaimed: *"He is the living God... His kingdom will not be destroyed, his dominion will never end... He has rescued Daniel."* (Daniel 6:26–27, NIV)

Yet **another international declaration** of God's supremacy resounded. The enemies who plotted Daniel's downfall were instead destroyed—illustrating that divine protection and justice honor the faithful. Darius' proclamation extended across the known world, echoing Nebuchadnezzar's earlier praise of God.

It is important to distinguish that Darius the Mede—governor appointed by Cyrus over former Babylonian territories (Daniel 5:31)—was a subordinate king to Cyrus the Persian, prophesied by Isaiah and Jeremiah. This layered royal testimony intensified God's glory and facilitated the divine decree allowing Israel's return from exile.

Daniel prospered under Darius and Cyrus. He had come to the place of the final prerequisite—the place where God desires all His servants to arrive: the realm of ultimate impact. His faithfulness, integrity, and sacrifice preserved God's people amid shifting global powers. When Daniel discerned through Jeremiah's prophecy the nearing end of Israel's seventy-year exile (Daniel 9:2), he interceded for his nation, catalyzing restoration.

God's principle remains:

- Sacrifice matures and qualifies the faithful.

- Divine deposits given in consecration are completed by tested faith.

- Promotion occurs in God's appointed time, for His glory and His people's good.

Daniel's journey shows that destiny fulfillment involves positioning oneself for Kingdom impact, transcending personal gain. His sacrifices became a platform from which God moved nations.

In the next chapter, we will delve into how Daniel's ultimate *becoming* ushered in prophecy's fulfillment and national restoration, revealing the broader divine design for all who walk the path of consecration, sacrifice, and divine appointment.

ESTHER – The Sacrifice of Courage and Divine Appointment

Esther, having transitioned into her sacrifice prerequisite, was now Queen over Persia—but she had not yet reached the final prerequisite. Like every stage, this phase carried a divinely appointed duration and layers within it. Esther was about to face its rigorous demands.

A deadly plot, born from Haman's hatred of her cousin Mordecai, threatened the entire Jewish race. The decree Haman secured from King Xerxes was irreversible—for in Persia, even the king could not revoke his own law.

Yet Mordecai's words rang with divine foresight: *"And who knows but that you have come to your royal position for such a time as this?"* (Esther 4:14, NIV)

This truth gradually dawned upon Esther. God, in His providence, had placed her as queen to act as an instrument of preservation for His people at a critical hour. Mordecai, serving as another instrument of divine transfer, stirred her toward the fulfillment of her destiny.

Responding with resolute faith, Esther called for a fast and prayer among the Jews. Fully aware of the danger—approaching the king unsummoned was punishable by death—she accepted the risk, laying down her life as a sacrifice for the sake of her people. This moment became her qualifying fire, proving her readiness to transition into the final prerequisite: divine appointment.

When Esther courageously entered the king's presence, he extended his royal scepter—a symbolic act of acceptance and pardon (Esther 5:2). That royal gesture marked her entrance into the ultimate realm of becoming—the place of anointing and destiny fulfillment.

Esther's Divine Strategy and Triumph

In this new realm, Esther did not hesitate. She strategically revealed Haman's plot, appealing directly to the king for her people's deliverance. Her courage and wisdom turned the king's heart, leading to Haman's downfall and the salvation of the Jews (Esther 7).

Through her obedience and sacrifice, Esther fulfilled her God-ordained purpose, demonstrating that the culmination of the journey to become brings not only personal elevation but also national preservation for believers in governmental seats of power.

Reflecting on the Pattern Bearers

Abraham became for the birthing of Israel and the salvation of the world. Jacob was shaped for the formation of Israel's nationhood and the coming of the Savior.

Joseph became the savior and steward of Egypt, preserving it—and many lives—through the famine. Moses became the deliverer of Israel, ushering them toward sovereignty.

David became king for Israel's protection, preparing the lineage of the Messiah. Esther became queen to save God's people from annihilation.

Each Pattern Bearer journeyed through the same prerequisites, every life a testament to the divine process of becoming—for a unique, redemptive purpose.

TRANSITIONING TO THE NEW TESTAMENT: The Principle Ascends

Principles, as we have emphasized, are not confined within the walls of time or context—they are eternal laws. The *Principle of Becoming* carries forward into the New Testament, where we encounter new pattern bearers who walk the same path—*primal consecration* and *sacrifice*—each preparing for their final prerequisite of *anointing*.

In this second part of the chapter, we will introduce these New Testament pattern bearers, tracing their journeys in chronological order. We will establish the foundation of *primal consecration* and *sacrifice prerequisites*, setting the stage for the ultimate prerequisite discussed in the next chapter.

Above all, the greatest Pattern Bearer—Jesus Christ—walked this path before us. For the sake of reconciling humanity to God, He passed through every prerequisite, culminating in supreme sacrifice upon the Cross and the glory of resurrection.

"He became poor, so that by his poverty he could make you rich." (2 Corinthians 8:9, NLT)

God did not spare Him but gave Him up for us all, that through His sacrifice we might have salvation and eternal life (Romans 8:32).

Jesus suffered and offered His perfect, sinless life to secure redemption for all. It is for the salvation of souls that God leads His servants through this journey of becoming—a divine process that molds them into vessels fit for eternal purpose.

As Scripture declares, God, wants every person to be saved and to come to a knowledge of the truth *(1 Timothy 2:3–4)*. Thus, this sacred journey is not reserved for a chosen few, but for all who heed the call to become—those who submit to His refining fire, yield to His process, and rise to serve as carriers of His glory.

For as it is written,

"What is happening now has happened before, and what will happen in the future has happened before, because God makes the same things happen over and over again." (Ecclesiastes 3:15, NLT)

The Principle of Becoming is timeless—repeated from generation to generation, perfected in Christ, and continued through those who follow Him.

JESUS AND THE PREREQUISITES: The Pattern of Divine Becoming

Jesus' Primal Consecration Prerequisite

From the very moment of His miraculous conception, Jesus was set apart for divine purpose. His primal consecration spanned approximately thirty years—a period marked by deliberate separation from worldly pursuits and deep immersion in divine preparation. This was not a passive phase but a foundational process in which the Son of God was sanctified, built up, and equipped for His ultimate mission.

His childhood, though largely obscure, was divinely orchestrated. It was a period of holy incubation—His season of hidden growth, formation, and consecration, akin to the primal preparation that all pattern bearers endure. He was circumcised on the eighth day, in alignment with the covenant established with Abraham—a mark of His participation in God's eternal promise. *(Genesis 17:12)*

As He matured, Scripture records: *"And Jesus grew in wisdom and stature, and in favor with God and men."* (Luke 2:52, NIV) His early life was one of purity, humility, diligence, and obedience—setting the stage for the unveiling of divine appointment.

The final act of His consecration came at His baptism by John the Baptist, who served as an *instrument of divine transfer*. As Jesus descended into the waters, the heavens opened and the Spirit of God rested upon Him like a dove. The voice of the Father declared: *"This is my Son, whom I love; with him I am well pleased."* (Matthew 3:17, NIV)

This divine affirmation sealed His consecration and transitioned Him into His second prerequisite—the realm of *sacrifice*. He laid down the anonymity and sanctity of His preparation to step fully into His divine calling.

Jesus' Sacrifice Prerequisite

The wilderness marked the beginning of Jesus' sacrifice prerequisite—a season of testing, temptation, and surrender of the flesh to the will of God. Just as every pattern bearer is refined through trial, this phase demanded complete obedience under extreme conditions.

For forty days and nights, He fasted and prayed, contending with the adversary. Satan's strategy focused on the threefold weakness of humanity: the lust of the flesh, the lust of the eyes, and the pride of life *(1 John 2:16)*.

First, Satan tempted Him through the *lust of the flesh*: *"If you are the Son of God, tell these stones to become bread."* (Matthew 4:3, NIV). The test sought to make Him use divine power for personal gratification. But Jesus replied: *"Man shall not live on bread alone, but by every word that proceeds from the mouth of God."* (Matthew 4:4, NKJV)

Next came the *pride of life*: *"Throw yourself down. For it is written: 'He will command his angels concerning you.'"* (Matthew 4:6, NIV). This was an invitation to perform for validation—to test the Father's protection and grasp glory before its appointed time. Jesus answered firmly: *"It is also written: 'Do not put the LORD your God to the test.'"* (Matthew 4:7)

Finally came the *lust of the eyes*: *"All this I will give you... if you will bow down and worship me."* (Matthew 4:9, NIV). The devil offered temporal dominion in exchange for worship. Jesus rebuked him: *"Away from me,*

Satan! For it is written: 'Worship the LORD your God, and serve him only.'" (Matthew 4:10, NIV).

These temptations represented the full assault on human weakness, yet Jesus triumphed through submission to divine authority. His obedience under pressure proved His maturity. His fast and victory purified the vessel and qualified Him for divine empowerment.

When the testing ended, *"Jesus returned to Galilee in the power of the Spirit."*(Luke 4:14, NIV). The sacrifice prerequisite had refined Him—He emerged strengthened, consecrated, and endowed with power for public ministry.

Jesus' Divine Appointment Prerequisite

Having overcome the tests of sacrifice, Jesus stepped into His final prerequisite—the divine appointment. His first public act was to declare His mission from the scroll of Isaiah:

"The Spirit of the LORD is on me, because he has anointed me to proclaim good news to the poor... to set the oppressed free, to proclaim the year of the LORD's favor."(Luke 4:18–19, NIV)

This was His formal unveiling—the beginning of divine authority manifested. His miracles validated the anointing: at Cana, He turned water into wine; He opened blind eyes, healed the sick, raised the dead, and commanded the elements of nature. His words carried divine authority, His presence manifested divine power.

Ultimately, the cross became the apex of His divine appointment—the place where the Son offered Himself as the perfect sacrifice. Scripture declares: He *"was declared with power to be the Son of God by his resurrection from the dead."* (Romans 1:4, NIV) Through death and resurrection, He attained the fullness of His appointment as Redeemer and King.

Jesus *became* through obedience, suffering, and sacrifice—ascending through each prerequisite to fulfill the will of the Father and establish eternal dominion.

The Pattern of Becoming in Christ

The life of Jesus affirms that the *Principle of Becoming* is divine, eternal, and immutable. His declaration— *"My food is to do the will of Him who sent Me, and to finish His work."* (John 4:34, NKJV)—reveals the heartbeat of the process. From primal consecration to sacrificial obedience and into divine appointment, His journey was a living manifestation of the Father's order for all who are called.

This pattern is our own divine roadmap. To *become* is to walk as He walked—through consecration, through sacrifice, and into divine appointment. It is the process by which vessels are refined for Kingdom authority, service, and eternal purpose.

Now, as we continue into the revelation of the final prerequisite—the age of divine appointment and anointing—we do so with the assurance that in Christ, this pattern reaches its perfection. The Son revealed it, the Apostles followed it, and every generation of believers is invited to live it.

Let us now turn to those who walked after Him, whose lives reflect the continuation of this holy process—the ongoing *Principle of Becoming* in the dispensation of grace.

THE 12 DISCIPLES and the Journey Through Consecration and Sacrifice

Primal Consecration: The Call to Follow

After Jesus' wilderness experience and His transition into the divine appointment prerequisite, He began gathering His disciples—those who would carry forward His mission and kingdom purposes. One by one, He called them from their everyday lives to a radical new journey marked by total surrender and transformation.

Among the first He called were Simon Peter and his brother Andrew, fishermen by trade. Jesus said simply, *"Come, follow me... and I will send you out to fish for people."* (Matthew 4:19, NIV) Without hesitation, they left their nets and families to follow Him. Shortly after, James and John, sons of Zebedee, were summoned and likewise abandoned their fishing business and father to become His followers *(Matthew 4:21–22)*.

These initial calls sparked a chain reaction; friends brought friends, families were left behind, and communities saw a growing group flocking to Jesus. To heed His call to follow marked the start of the disciples' primal consecration prerequisite—a season of setting apart their lives completely for God's unfolding plan.

Spiritual Formation and Training

The years that followed were foundational. Walking with Jesus, the disciples experienced intense spiritual formation; their primal consecration was nurtured through teaching, correction, and direct participation in Jesus' ministry.

Jesus equipped them through parables—divine lessons layered with spiritual truth—and answered their deepest questions about the kingdom of God. He taught them to pray when requested *(Luke 11:1–4)*, modeled holiness, obedience, and servant leadership. In this time, they matured in spirit, character, and knowledge, gradually shedding old worldly perspectives.

As Jesus prepared to complete His public ministry, the disciples' season of primal consecration was drawing to a close. They were being prepared for the greater demands of sacrifice.

The Sacrifice Prerequisite: Trial and Transformation

The sacrifice prerequisite for the disciples began poignantly after Christ's resurrection. Over the next 40 days, Jesus appeared intermittently—sometimes present, sometimes gone—creating a raw tension in their hearts and faith. This shift tested their walk profoundly.

Peter's struggle epitomized this trial. Familiar with Peter's impetuous personality, after discovering him fishing once again, Jesus asked thrice: *"Simon son of John, do you love me?"* (John 21:17, NIV) Each time Peter affirmed his love, Jesus replied with a command: *"Feed my lambs." "Take care of my sheep." "Feed my sheep."*

This sacred exchange was more than restoration—it was a commission, defining Peter's core mission as the Divine Shepherd's caretaker of the flock. This moment was a profound purification and preparation—a test breaking Peter's heart to rebuild it in divine service.

The Heart of the Journey: Becoming for the Flock

This testing and transformation highlight the core goal of the Principle of Becoming: to be of utmost effect in advancing God's kingdom, not for self-glory but for the salvation and restoration of souls—the poor, needy, vulnerable, and voiceless. We become for them.

Only upon entering the final prerequisite do we receive the authority and power, like the pattern bearers before us, to influence and heal a broken, corrupted world that oppresses the weak. It's a call to arise, fully equipped, fully surrendered, and fully empowered to serve.

The Promise of Empowerment

Before Jesus ascended, He charged His disciples with the Great Commission *(Matthew 28:18–20)* but sent them back to Jerusalem with a vital command:

"Do not leave Jerusalem, but wait for the gift my Father promised, which you have heard me speak about… in a few days you will be baptized with the Holy Spirit." (Acts 1:4–5, NIV)

He understood that despite their preparation, they lacked the power necessary for global impact. His own triumph over sacrifice had equipped Him to receive the power of the Spirit; He now told them to mirror the same pattern.

The Upper Room and Pentecost: The Infilling of Power

For ten days, the disciples gathered in prayerful unity—waiting and interceding. This upper room experience was more than a waiting period; it was the qualifying fire for their final prerequisite. They faced uncertainty, longing, and anticipation, having left behind much to follow.

On Pentecost, a supernatural outpouring unleashed transforming power:

"Suddenly a sound like the blowing of a violent wind came from heaven and filled the whole house... They saw what seemed to be tongues of fire that separated and came to rest on each of them. All of them were filled with the Holy Spirit and began to speak in other tongues as the Spirit enabled them." (Acts 2:2–4, NIV)

Clothed in this power, the once-fearful disciples became bold proclaimers of the gospel. Peter, once cowardly and denying Christ, preached fervently, and 3,000 souls were added that day to them (Acts 2:41).

Walking in Anointing and Divine Appointment

From Pentecost onward, the disciples manifested miracles, healing, signs, and wonders—hallmarks of their entry into the final prerequisite: anointing and divine appointment. Their faithful endurance of the sacrifice prerequisite positioned them to carry God's purposes with authority.

This journey of the disciples encapsulates the Principle of Becoming: a path beginning with consecration, tested and refined by sacrifice, culminating in divine anointing and appointment for kingdom advancement.

In the next chapter, we will explore this final prerequisite further, unpacking the fullness of divine empowerment and destiny that marks the true fulfillment of becoming.

APOSTLE PAUL and the Prerequisites: The Path of Divine Becoming

Primal Consecration: The Casting of the Holy Fire

The transformation of Saul, the zealous persecutor of the early church, into Apostle Paul, the greatest missionary of the gospel, begins with a profound encounter—one that marked the end of his persecutor days and heralded the beginning of his primal consecration.

On his journey to Damascus, Saul was violently determined to eradicate the followers of Christ. Suddenly, a blinding light from heaven enveloped him, and the voice of Christ thundered: *"Saul, Saul, why do you persecute me?"* (Acts 9:4, NIV)

This encounter was not merely a physical confrontation but a spiritual turning point—an imminent call to primal consecration. Saul fell to the ground, blinded by the divine light, and was led into Damascus, where Ananias, acting as an instrument of divine transfer, was sent to him. Ananias laid hands on Saul, and scales fell from his eyes. Saul's eyes were opened not just physically but spiritually—he received a new vision, a divine purpose. His old zeal for destruction was replaced with zeal for Christ, and his heart was set apart for divine service.

Barnabas, a key instrument of divine transfer himself, introduced Saul to the disciples in Jerusalem, affirming his genuine conversion: *"Barnabas took him and brought him to the apostles. He told them how Saul on his journey had seen the Lord and that the Lord had spoken to him"* (Acts 9:27, NIV).

This divine connection cemented Saul's place in the community, but it was only the beginning. The crucial, foundational principle of primal consecration—an initial deposit of faith, purpose, and divine encounter—had been laid. Saul's transformation was complete, but his journey of becoming was only beginning.

The Three Years in Arabia: Spirit-Driven Foundation

Paul recognized that true effectivity in God's kingdom required more than initial salvation and calling. In Galatians, he recounts:

"I did not go up to Jerusalem to see those who were apostles before I was, but I went into Arabia. Later I returned to Damascus. Then after three years, I went up to Jerusalem to get acquainted with Peter and stayed with him fifteen days." (Galatians 1:17-18, NIV)

For three years, Paul remained in Arabia—hidden, secluded, but transformed. This season of primal consecration was vital. It was during this time that he received divine revelations directly from Christ Himself, as he wrote: *"I want you to know, brothers and sisters, that the gospel I preached is not of human origin. I did not receive it from any man, nor was I taught it; rather, I received it by revelation from Jesus Christ."* (Galatians 1:11–12, NIV)

These three years represented a divine deposit—growth in the Spirit, deepening of capacity, and the internalization of the gospel message. This period was crucial; it was the foundation upon which everything else would be built. In this hidden wilderness, Paul's spiritual maturity was forged—he was being equipped for the next levels of divine service.

Paul also affirmed saying God, revealed *"his Son in me so that I might preach him among the Gentiles."* (Galatians 1:16, NIV) It was the sacred place of primal consecration, where internal structures for effective kingdom work were laid solid.

The Sacrifice Prerequisite: The Mission of Antioch

In Acts, the Holy Spirit explicitly directed: *"Set apart for me Barnabas and Saul for the work to which I have called them."* (Acts 13:2, NIV)

The journey of sacrifice truly commenced as Paul and Barnabas launched their first missionary journey, marked in Acts 13–14. After leaving Antioch, they faced relentless opposition, hardship, and persecution. They endured shipwrecks, imprisonment, and hostility from both Jews and Gentiles. These trials were the fiery furnace—tests of flesh and spirit—that refined Paul's purpose and character.

Paul and Barnabas encountered fierce opposition in cities like Iconium, Lystra, and Derbe, yet they pressed on, preaching the gospel, planting churches, and trusting God's power. *"They preached the gospel in that city and won a large number of disciples."* (Acts 14:21, NIV)

Their obedience and sacrifices bore fruit—signs, wonders, and lasting communities. But their journey was not merely physical; it was a sacrifice of comfort, fame, and personal ambition. As Paul journeyed here, he forsook worldly gain to fulfill divine mandates—this was the sacrifice prerequisite in action.

The culmination of this journey came when Paul and Barnabas returned to Antioch, reporting how God had opened doors through much suffering. Paul's sacrifice proved he was qualified for the next stage—the final prerequisite: anointing and divine appointment.

The Transition to the Final Prerequisite

Having experienced unceasing trials and victories in his sacrifice prerequisite in the journey to become, Paul and Barnabas returned, marking the end of this phase for Paul. Their eventual separation ushered in a divine transition—one ordained by God to propel Paul into greater dimensions of purpose.

"They had such a sharp disagreement that they parted company. Barnabas took Mark and sailed for Cyprus, but Paul chose Silas and left, commended by the believers to the grace of the Lord." (Acts 15:39–40, NIV)

This divine manipulation of circumstance—though appearing as conflict—was in fact a strategic separation. It positioned Paul for the highest level of influence and divine empowerment. In this separation, this divine transfer, Paul was moved into the ultimate realm of his calling—postured for the fullness of divine destiny.

After this point, Paul's ministry exploded, growing in impact and force. The Scriptures testify: *"God did extraordinary miracles through Paul."* (Acts 19:11, NIV)

He had come into the final prerequisite—the divine appointment—where his ministry carried global influence, supernatural authority, and eternal fruit.

Moving Forward

As we reflect on the lives of the apostles, we realize that their stories echo the same divine pattern: consecration, sacrifice, and appointment. The Principle of Becoming is unchanging. It is embedded in Scripture as the divine law for all who are called to carry their generation's weight and to fulfill their unique destiny in God's eternal plan.

In the next chapter, we will delve deeper into the significance of the final prerequisite—**anointing and divine appointment**—and reveal how the maturities cultivated through sacrifice prepare us to influence and heal this broken world, firmly establishing that the end of every process is always greater than the beginning.

THE PREREQUISITES: CONSECRATION, SACRIFICE, AND DIVINE APPOINTMENT—A FOUNDATIONAL JOURNEY

It is crucial to recognize that these stages—the prerequisites—do not replace each other but build upon one another continuously. We are called to live lives perpetually marked by consecration and sacrifice, even after being divinely appointed in the final prerequisite, as we fulfill the ultimate purpose of our lives. The initial two prerequisites serve as the essential foundation—building the **character of consecration** and the **mentality of sacrifice**. These become a lifestyle necessary for thriving in the final prerequisite.

Hebrews 2:10 (NKJV) declares:

"For it was fitting for Him, for whom are all things and by whom are all things, in bringing many sons to glory, to make the captain of their salvation perfect through sufferings."

This perfection through suffering is the training of the **sacrifice prerequisite**. Through this refining fire, you are brought into maturity and glory. Christ has already endured this journey for you—but you must walk through it as well, to be brought fully into glory.

Salvation is foundational, but not the end. It is the door that opens the path. You may choose to remain at the threshold with mere profession of faith, yet never fully function in the Kingdom of God. Many settle in comfort, afraid to venture deeper into God's will due to fear of the cost. But the journey demands sacrifice; no comfort zone should become a resting place. Your refuge must be God Himself, and the pursuit of more of Him your ultimate goal.

The sacrifice prerequisite, as seen in the stories of the pattern-bearers, pushes you beyond comfort and keeps you on holy edge. Yet surrendering fully to God's will conquers this prerequisite and leads to advancement into the next realm of becoming. Scripture exhorts:

"Work out your salvation with fear and trembling." (Philippians 2:12, NIV) *"Be all the more eager to make your calling and election sure."* (2 Peter 1:10, NIV)

Remember—**salvation is not the endgame; it is the beginning of God's plan in you.**

The Fellowship of His Sufferings: The Pathway into Maturity

"For it was fitting for Him, for whom are all things and by whom are all things, in bringing many sons to glory, to make the captain of their salvation perfect through sufferings." (Hebrews 2:10, NKJV)

Perfected through suffering. This suffering is the training in the Sacrifice Prerequisite. You are being perfected. You are brought into glory by this training. You are matured. He has gone through the brood for you already. You don't have to. But He must bring you to the **same glory**. The objective was higher than your receiving Salvation. That was foundational. Not final. You must be brought into glory. That is; In this life.

The sacrifice prerequisite is the divine classroom where the Holy Spirit inducts you into the mysteries of Christ's own journey. It is not random pain, but intentional formation. It is the stripping away of all that competes with the nature of Christ within you. It is the laying down of every weight—seen and unseen—that hinders your ascent into mature sonship. Through this holy training, you are shaped, refined, and forged for the glory you were destined to carry.

For this reason Paul cried out:

"that I may know Him and the power of His resurrection, and the fellowship of His sufferings, being conformed to His death," (Philippians 3:10, NKJV)

To cause you to Mature, God brings you into His Fellowship. That is, the Fellowship of His sufferings. We suffer like He suffered. A customised cup of suffering specific to You. Problem is, we retreat. This is the sacrifice Prerequisite.

The Place of the Cross that you may know God more intimately. This is how the many names of God came about. In a place of suffering the revelations of God are brought to a more intimate level. It's the fellowship of His sufferings. There is no shortcut. But it doesn't end there.

Sacrifice is not merely endurance; it is revelation. In the place of your deepest pressing, God unveils Himself at His deepest level. Every patriarch, every prophet, every pattern-bearer received their revelation names of God in the fire of affliction. Likewise, your suffering becomes the sacred chamber where God reveals Himself to you as He truly is—not by theory, but by encounter.

Peter affirms this sanctifying process:

"Therefore, since Christ suffered for us in the flesh, arm yourselves also with the same mind, for he who has suffered in the flesh has ceased from sin, that he no longer should live the rest of his time in the flesh for the lusts of men, but for the will of God." (1 Peter 4:1–2, NKJV)

The suffering in the flesh is supposed to lead you to be conformed to His death. Until this death happens, the suffering continues. The death of the self-life. The breaking of self promotion, self preservation, and self gratification. When God sees death, the suffering stops. When you are conformed to His death because of the fellowship of suffering, you come to the level of power.

This is the mystery: **God ends the suffering when it produces death—death to self, and life unto God.** Only then does the next realm open. Only then does power descend and rest upon you without measure. This is why the fellowship of His sufferings is the doorway into the power of His resurrection, a virtue of the final prerequisite—Anointing.

The Principle of the Prerequisites in the Journey to Become is simply an eagle eye scope view of the journey to maturity in Christ as taught by the True and inerrant word of God. The place of mature sonship. Sacrifice, therefore, is not punishment; it is promotion. It is not abandonment; it is alignment. It is not the end of you; it is the beginning of Him formed fully within you. Through this holy prerequisite, God does not reduce you—He reveals you. He brings you into glory.

Rise up—do not merely warm pews. The days are latter, the harvest is plentiful, but the workers are few. God requires that the faithful few who, having journeyed through the prerequisites, will be entrusted with power and authority to advance His Kingdom for the salvation of souls. Paul begins his letter to the Ephesians with these powerful words:

"Paul, an apostle of Christ Jesus by the will of God, to God's holy people in Ephesus, the faithful in Christ Jesus: Grace and peace to you from God our Father and the Lord Jesus Christ.

Praise be to the God and Father of our Lord Jesus Christ, who has blessed us in the heavenly realms with every spiritual blessing in Christ. For He chose us in Him before the creation of the world to be holy and blameless in His sight. In love He predestined us for adoption to sonship through Jesus Christ, in accordance with His pleasure and will—to the praise of His glorious grace." (Ephesians 1:1–6, NIV)

The journey into conformity with Christ begins when you **capture your true identity**. Just as Jacob could not proceed into the promised land until his name was changed to Israel, you too cannot mature and fulfill your purpose until you embrace your God-ordained identity in Christ.

The sacrifice prerequisite is the process of breaking the self to achieve greater glory, effective service, and profound Kingdom work. It is the highest expression of love—laying down one's life for God's purposes and the advancement of His Kingdom. Jesus Himself declared:

"Greater love has no one than this: to lay down one's life for one's friends." (John 15:13, NIV)

Paul echoed this same truth:

"Now I rejoice in what I am suffering for you, and I fill up in my flesh what is still lacking in regard to Christ's afflictions, for the sake of His body, which is the church." (Colossians 1:24–25, NIV)

Though pruning is painful, it yields righteous fruit:

"No discipline seems pleasant at the time, but painful. Later on, however, it produces a harvest of righteousness and peace for those who have been trained by it." (Hebrews 12:11, NIV)

Sacrifice pleases God:

"Through Jesus, therefore, let us continually offer to God a sacrifice of praise—the fruit of lips that openly profess His name. And do not forget to do good and to share with others, for with such sacrifices God is pleased." (Hebrews 13:15–16, NIV)

The journey to become is intentional and demands that your sacrifices be consecrated and pure. Like the Old Testament priests who washed themselves before entering the Holy of Holies, you too must be set apart. *(Leviticus 1:9)"Therefore, I urge you, brothers and sisters, in view of God's mercy, to offer your bodies as a living sacrifice, holy and pleasing to God—this is your true and proper worship."* (Romans 12:1, NIV)

God will not advance anyone to the final prerequisite without the foundation of intentional consecration and sacrifice.

Only the steadfast remain on the journey. Just as the disciples who gathered in the upper room dwindled to a faithful few by the tenth day, so it is on the path of becoming. Even during their primal consecration, they asked, *'What will we have?'* for leaving all to follow Christ *(Matthew 19:27)*. Jesus promised:

"Everyone who has left houses or brothers or sisters or father or mother or wife or children or fields for my sake will receive a hundred times as much and will inherit eternal life." (Matthew 19:29, NIV)

Their sacrifice was never in vain.

Life is a process of pursuit toward destiny fullness. Scripture warns:

"If you falter in a time of trouble, how small is your strength!" (Proverbs 24:10, NIV). So gird your loins and be courageous.

"When people do not accept divine guidance, they run wild. But whoever obeys the law is joyful." (Proverbs 29:18, NLT)

By embracing divine guidance and the laws of becoming, your latter days will end in joy. Accept the journey's demands. Become a vessel of highest effect in God's hand—a royal diadem and battle axe of righteousness.

The Principle of Becoming—consecration, sacrifice, and divine appointment—is the unchanging divine law *for all who are called to impact their generation and beyond. The path is arduous, but the glory released is immeasurable and eternal.*

PREREQUISITE THREE: ANOINTING: DIVINE APPOINTMENT

This stage—the final prerequisite—is the place of **anointing and divine appointment**. All prior preparation, testing, and refining reach their culmination here. Now it is time to rise and step fully into the purpose for which God has prepared you.

God is not one who trains on the job; He forges mature vessels through seasons of preparation and proves their readiness for the weight of responsibility. At this point, you are perfectly positioned for divine deployment—a tried, trustworthy, and reliable instrument in the hand of the

Master. Having journeyed through consecration and sacrifice, you have now matured into the stature of *huios*—the son of loving maturity—able to raise others, to serve selflessly, and to sacrifice for the gain of others, even when no gain comes to you.

Here, the distinction of being chosen transcends mere calling. Having walked faithfully through the first two prerequisites, you now arrive at the place of function and availability—ready to move in the specific dimension of influence to which God has called you. This is the realm where destiny and divine empowerment converge, producing a vessel through which God can effect transformation and establish His Kingdom order.

In this chapter, we will examine the impact of this final prerequisite in the lives of the pattern bearers we have studied—from Abraham to Paul—and draw forth the profound truths revealed through their journeys. Observing the repeated patterns of **preparation, testing, and empowerment** confirms the authenticity of this divine principle. The successful navigation of this final step validates it as a tested law of spiritual growth and divine service.

Yet more than a position or a gift, this final prerequisite is a revelation of divine nature—a maturing into the fullness of love and compassion, even toward the undeserving. This is the realm of **loving maturity**—the essence that defines true divine appointment. Here, you learn to love as Christ loves: overlooking faults, extending grace, and cultivating a deep, transformative compassion that governs every decision and response.

Divine appointment is not merely an honor; it is a **sacred stewardship**, borne of obedience, sacrifice, and spiritual growth. It is the unveiling of divine intent—the moment when what God placed within you finds its ultimate expression. In this stage, the journey to become reaches its highest summit. The immeasurable power of God flows through vessels refined by process, vessels who have endured the fire and emerged as bearers of His glory—ordained to touch generations and fulfill eternal purposes.

As we proceed, we will explore how this final stage shaped and propelled each pattern bearer beyond who they were into who they were destined to become—the mantle of God's glory resting firmly upon them, advancing His Kingdom in miraculous and undeniable ways.

ABRAHAM: Fulfillment Through Becoming

Having completed and satisfied his sacrifice prerequisite—demonstrating unwavering allegiance, love, and steadfast commitment to prioritize God's will above human comfort and instinct—Abraham could now rest assured that God's promises to him were certain and secure.

With his sacrifice prerequisite fulfilled, his focus turned toward securing Isaac's legacy and ensuring that his seed would continue to fulfill God's promises after his departure. This sacred responsibility defined Abraham's final prerequisite—the place of divine appointment and destiny fulfillment.

As a prudent and wise pattern bearer, Abraham took deliberate steps to steward this phase well. He ensured that Isaac was joined to Rebekah, the wife ordained by God from among Abraham's own people, through the servant's faithful mission recorded in *Genesis chapter 24.* This act was crucial in safeguarding the divine covenant and securing the continuation of God's redemptive plan through Abraham's lineage.

Abraham's death, recorded in *Genesis 25:7–8,* came after a long and fruitful life: *"Abraham lived a hundred and seventy-five years. Then Abraham breathed his last and died at a good old age, an old man and full of years; and he was gathered to his people."* (Genesis 25:7–8, NIV)

This account highlights not only his longevity but the satisfaction and fullness of life he attained—a testimony to the great reward of journeying faithfully through the prerequisites to become. The reward transcends the pain of process, filling the soul with deep gratitude, peace, and divine completion.

Reaching this point of destiny fullness—*the place of becoming*—is to stand in the realm of anointing and divine appointment, where one's ultimate purpose of creation is realized. Through Abraham's faithful obedience, God's grand redemptive plan advanced significantly. His life of consecration and sacrifice birthed a chosen nation—**Israel**—through whom the Savior of the world would come.

The profundity of Abraham's journey lies in its eternal impact: by fulfilling his divine purpose, he did not merely bless a family but established the foundation for the Kingdom of Light to prevail over darkness. Through his seed, the Messiah, Jesus Christ, entered history to reconcile humanity to God. In this light, Abraham's becoming represents a vital and indelible piece of the divine order—a sacred legacy that reshaped the course of human destiny.

This pattern of becoming—moving through consecration, sacrifice, and divine appointment—embodies God's method for raising those who will carry forth His Kingdom purposes.

Abraham stands as a timeless witness that the fulfillment of one's calling is never personal alone but contributes directly to the unfolding of God's eternal plan of salvation and restoration upon the earth.

JACOB & JOSEPH: Father and Son in the Becoming Journey

The Culmination of Loving-Maturity

Loving-maturity is the crowning byproduct of faithfully traversing all spiritual prerequisites. This maturity is not merely age or experience—it is a deep, supernatural capacity to transcend human offense and embrace divine compassion. It is the place where one is no longer bound by bitterness or the need for vindication, but instead becomes so filled with God's heart that mercy and compassion overflow—even toward those who have done harm.

Loving-maturity "keeps no record of wrongs" and "always trusts, always hopes, always perseveres" (*1 Corinthians 13:4–8, NIV*).

This Christlike love is forged in the fire of the journey to become—refined and revealed most fully in the final prerequisite: anointing and divine appointment.

The Interwoven Journeys: Joseph's Elevation & Jacob's Fulfillment

After Joseph had navigated the valleys and fires of his own journey, rising as Egypt's grand vizier and stepping into his final prerequisite, God purposed to use him as the very instrument of divine transfer for his father Jacob *(now called Israel)*. Joseph's readiness, wisdom, and proven character positioned him not only to preserve Egypt but also to fulfill God's promise to his father— "I will make you a great nation" (*Genesis 46:3*).

Joseph's process was swift, designed to prepare him quickly as a deliverer, because he would help carry his father into destiny fullness. For Jacob, whose destiny was to birth a nation, the process was longer; greater assignments often require deeper and more protracted refinement.

While Joseph functioned in Egypt as second only to Pharaoh, the famine raged in Canaan, pressing Jacob toward the culmination of his own sacrifice prerequisite.

Joseph's foresight and stewardship ensured there was grain when none could be found elsewhere, leading his brothers *(unaware of his true identity)* to Egypt for sustenance.

Joseph, now clothed in Egyptian splendor, did not reveal himself immediately. Instead, he tested his brothers, seeking evidence of repentance and transformation in their hearts—an essential step, since the destinies of all Israel's tribes rested upon their character.

Meanwhile, Jacob in Canaan confronted his greatest fears as famine pressed him to send his precious sons to Egypt—first withholding and then, at Joseph's demand, surrendering Benjamin, the beloved. The pain echoed Abraham's willingness to offer up Isaac, demanding that Jacob too surrender what he cherished most for the sake of God's larger promise. This surrender—this willingness to let go—was Jacob's qualifying fire.

Scripture describes this sacred stewardship of sons: *"Sons are a heritage from the LORD, children a reward from him. Like arrows in the hands of a warrior are sons born in one's youth. Blessed is the man whose quiver is full of them. They will not be put to shame when they contend with their enemies in the gate."* (Psalm 127:3–5, NIV)

For Jacob, the risk of losing sons was a deep trial—for his sons represented both his security and his legacy.

Divine Transfer: The Reunion and New Beginning

After Joseph's tests revealed a true change in his brothers, he made himself known to them:

"I am your brother Joseph, the one you sold into Egypt! And now, do not be distressed and do not be angry with yourselves for selling me here, because it was to save lives that God sent me ahead of you." (Genesis 45:4–8, NIV)

It was a forgiving, embracing, and redemptive moment—a perfect display of *loving-maturity*. Joseph saw divine purpose even in the wrongs done against him, perceiving the sovereignty and goodness of God in all things.

Joseph then became the instrument of divine transfer for Jacob. He invited his father to dwell in the best part of Egypt, Goshen, safeguarding the new nation's future: *"You shall dwell in the land of Goshen... there I will provide for you."* (Genesis 45:10–11, NKJV)

Pharaoh confirmed this blessing, granting Jacob's clan the choicest land and abundant provision. Revived by the good news, Jacob moved his family to Egypt, entering his final prerequisite—the place of destiny fulfillment, where God's promise to make him a nation would finally flourish.

In the safe 'womb' of Egypt, the family of Israel grew, and the twelve sons—patriarchs of the tribes—began to multiply further.

Blessing, Legacy, and the Fruit of Loving-Maturity

Before his death, Jacob's life reached its zenith. He pronounced prophetic blessings over each of his sons, finalizing their callings and setting the course for Israel's future—mirroring Abraham's blessing upon Isaac.

"When Jacob had finished giving instructions to his sons, he drew his feet up into the bed, breathed his last, and was gathered to his people." (Genesis 49:33, NIV)

He died full of years, satisfied, having seen God's faithfulness.

Yet Joseph's loving-maturity shone brightest after Jacob's passing. Fearing retribution, his brothers pleaded for forgiveness, but Joseph—now a fully "become" man—responded with transcendent grace:

"Don't be afraid. Am I in the place of God? You intended to harm me, but God intended it for good... the saving of many lives. So then, don't be afraid. I will provide for you and your children." And he reassured them and spoke kindly to them." (Genesis 50:19–21, NIV)

Loving-maturity, as revealed in Joseph, is the divine ability to release the past, extend mercy, and serve the redemptive plan—no matter the personal cost. It is the essence of Christlike love:

"Love is patient, love is kind. It does not envy, it does not boast, it is not proud... It keeps no record of wrongs... always trusts, always hopes, always perseveres. Love never fails." (1 Corinthians 13:4–8, NIV)

This is the fruit of the journey to become. In loving-maturity, every wound is transformed into wisdom, every wrong into an opportunity for grace. It is the highest proof of divine appointment, and the surest sign that one has truly *become.*

From here, we proceed to explore loving-maturity and final becoming through the life of Moses, as the divine pattern of transformation continues to unfold.

MOSES: Exemplifying Loving-Maturity in Leadership

Moses, fully established in his final prerequisite, stood as the leader of the entire nation of Israel throughout their wilderness journey to the Promised Land. His relationship with God had deepened profoundly—characterized by intimate communication where *"the LORD would speak to Moses face to face, as one speaks to a friend"* (Exodus 33:11, NIV). Moses frequently ascended Mount Sinai for extended periods to commune with God directly. (Exodus 24:18).

His loving-maturity is powerfully shown in his intercession for the people. When the Israelites sinned grievously, God's anger burned hot, threatening to destroy them and start anew with Moses Himself:

"Now leave me alone so that my anger may burn against them and that I may destroy them. Then I will make you into a great nation." (Exodus 32:10, NIV)

In response, Moses stood in the gap with intercession, even later pleading passionately:

"But now, please forgive their sin—but if not, then blot me out of the book you have written." (Exodus 32:32, NIV)

This selfless intercession reveals a man whose love transcended personal pain and disappointment. The people Moses led were stiff-necked, rebellious, and burdensome—causing him tremendous distress—yet he unflinchingly offered his very life for their sake. That is the essence of loving-maturity: putting the needs and eternity of others above self.

When the LORD decreed He would no longer dwell among the people due to their idolatry, Moses acted decisively. He erected the Tent of Meeting as a sacred place for God's presence to commune with Israel, serving as the pivotal intercessory hub that preserved the nation's relationship with God despite their sin (*Exodus 33:7–11*). Moses' demand was resolute:

"If Your Presence does not go with us, do not send us up from here." (Exodus 33:15, NIV)

This steadfastness—his refusal to separate God from the people—epitomizes the highest expression of spiritual maturity: *loving-maturity.* Taking responsibility for a people, forgiving, interceding, and seeking God's presence continually are marks of a fully 'become' leader. Such maturity cannot be faked or rushed; it is the product of the journey through all prior prerequisites. The first two—primal consecration and sacrifice—are non-negotiable foundations for the final fruitful stage of divine appointment.

Moses' humility remains unmatched in Scripture: *"Now Moses was a very humble man, more humble than anyone else on the face of the earth." (Numbers 12:3, NIV)*

His humility came not from weakness but from the profound humbling experiences he endured across his journey—years in exile, rejection, leading a stiff-necked nation, and continual intercession before God. The divine appointment prerequisite—though a place of great authority and intimacy with God—carries a learning curve in which humility remains paramount.

Even as leader of a nation and God's mouthpiece, Moses humbly accepted counsel. When Jethro, his father-in-law, advised him to delegate the judging of minor disputes to others, Moses listened and implemented the wisdom, creating structures to sustain leadership and ministry (*Exodus 18:13–24*). This submission to guidance despite his elevated position is a clear sign of spiritual maturity and wisdom; pride was nowhere to be found.

As we close Moses' story, we learn that becoming is not merely about rising in rank but growing in heart—to love as God loves. By moving through consecration, sacrifice, and divine appointment, Moses became the shepherd a leaderless people desperately needed. His life stands as testimony that God's making process equips vessels to carry His redemptive work forward—extending His grace, power, and love to multitudes.

This pattern is immutable yet consistent: every genuine becoming carries eternal impact, advancing God's kingdom through holy love and faithful service.

PREREQUISITES AND THE REFINING FIRE: THE JOURNEY TO BECOME

The journey through the prerequisites of consecration, sacrifice, and divine appointment mirrors perfectly the refining process of silver described in *Malachi 3:3 (NIV)*: *"He will sit as a refiner and purifier of silver; he will purify the Levites and refine them like gold and silver."*

This powerful analogy reveals the nature of God's transformative work in the life of every believer called to become. Just as a skilled silversmith holds the silver piece over the hottest part of the fire, God carefully and continually refines His people. The silversmith's eyes remain fixed on the silver throughout the process—the refining cannot go too long lest the silver be damaged or destroyed, nor too short lest impurities remain.

Likewise, God allows trials, testing, and purification in measured doses—never permitting destruction but always demanding sanctification.

The goal of this divine refining process is that when God looks upon His people, He sees His own image reflected clearly in them—the image of Christ, pure, righteous, and mature. This is the ultimate becoming—not simply survival through the fire, but emerging fully refined for God's purpose.

Hebrews 12:11 (NIV) underscores this vital truth about refining through trials: *"No discipline seems pleasant at the time, but painful. Later on, however, it produces a harvest of righteousness and peace for those who have been trained by it."*

The 'discipline' mentioned here is the encompassing experience of the prerequisites' refining fires. Consecration purifies the heart and sets us apart. The sacrifice prerequisite burns away the natural instincts and false securities of the flesh, shaping obedience and surrender.

The final prerequisite completes the process—ushering us into a life of divine power, wisdom, and loving-maturity.

This is not a quick or easy process, but it is one perfectly designed by God Himself. The product of this alchemical journey is a vessel of great value—like pure silver shining brilliantly in the light of God's glory, ready and worthy for Kingdom service. This final-refined state marks the 'having become' quality God demands for those being raised to positions of authority and trust.

Just like the silversmith who knows the silver is ready when his own reflection is perfectly visible on its surface, so also the LORD knows the heart that is perfectly faithful when it mirrors His love, humility, and righteousness. This is what it means to truly become—to be made fully ready and fit for His divine purposes, bearing the marks of both struggle and victory.

The analogy and the scriptural principles align seamlessly to describe the essence of the journey to become: a divine, attentive refining that produces mature vessels—vessels that can carry God's glory into every dimension of life.

Understanding this refining process should encourage every believer walking the path of becoming. ***Though the trials seem arduous, their outcome is immeasurably glorious***—*transformation into the likeness of Christ, prepared for divine appointment and eternal impact.*

THE JOURNEY OF DAVID: Fulfillment, Power, and the Continued Call to Discipline

Having completed the season of sacrifice and endured its refining fires, David returned to Judah, where he was crowned king. After seven years of ruling Judah, he was anointed king over the united nation of Israel—God's promise fulfilled in full measure. At this pinnacle, David entered the place of destiny's fullness, the final prerequisite—the place of *becoming*—where God intended him to reign.

In this season, David accomplished remarkable feats. He captured Jerusalem, making it both the political and spiritual capital of Israel. Peace and prosperity surrounded the borders, and the promises once spoken to Abraham took tangible form under David's reign. The land flourished, enemies were subdued, and the nation grew strong and fruitful. David even brought the Ark of the Covenant to Jerusalem, marking God's abiding presence and favor.

Through the prophet Nathan, God made a covenant that would echo through eternity:

"I will raise up your offspring to succeed you, your own flesh and blood, and I will establish his kingdom... Your house and your kingdom will endure forever before me; your throne will be established forever."(2 Samuel 7:12–16, NIV)

David's alignment in this final prerequisite signified that he had become a vessel flowing with divine power—a chosen leader strengthened by the process of becoming. His victories multiplied, and the blessing of God rested mightily upon him.

Growing Power and Maturity

David's authority expanded—not only in dominion, but in grace and spiritual depth. Though the same shepherd boy who once faced Goliath, the fires of the journey to become had transformed him. His capacity, wisdom, and power had matured through the process.

Power—spiritual or natural*—is never given all at once. It is accumulated through obedience. At every stage of consecration, sacrifice, and becoming, God adds grace, strength, and divine ability.*

David's Struggles: The Necessity of Steadfast Discipline

Arrival at destiny does not conclude the journey—it intensifies it. Consecration and sacrifice are not seasonal acts; they are lifelong disciplines. David's life demonstrates this truth.

In his earlier years, David was unwavering—disciplined in purity and obedience. When fleeing Saul, he upheld holiness, even when eating the sacred showbread to survive (Leviticus 24:5–9; 1 Samuel 21:4–6). Yet later, in his kingship, that discipline weakened.

The Bathsheba scandal revealed a lapse in consecration. Though forgiven, the ripple effects of that sin brought devastating consequences. At the height of divine appointment, even small breaches carry weighty costs. Unaddressed impurity, left to fester, can undermine anointing.

The consistent truth remains: consecration and sacrifice must be renewed continually. They are safeguards against decay. As wine is refined through repeated pourings, so must the believer's heart be purified again and again until no trace of corruption remains.

Pride—the sin that destroyed Saul—lurks near power. David's error was not only moral but vocational. He abandoned the duties of kingship, sending others to battle while he stayed behind. Neglect of calling is itself a breach of consecration. Though repentance restored him, the lesson endures: discipline and humility are the foundation stones of enduring power.

The Enemy's Warfare and the Need for Vigilance

Even in high spiritual places, the enemy seeks to destroy.

"Be self-controlled and alert your enemy the devil prowls around like a roaring lion looking for someone to devour." (1 Peter 5:8, NIV)

Satan aims to undermine progress and corrupt calling. Thus, Scripture warns:

"He who digs a pit will fall into it, and whoever breaks through a wall will be bitten by a serpent." (Ecclesiastes 10:8, NKJV)

Consecration and sacrifice act as walls of divine protection—spiritual fortifications that preserve those advancing in the Kingdom. Until Christ's return, we remain both pilgrims and warriors, called to hold the line with vigilance, clothed in God's promises and power.

A Final Moment of Humbling

Near the end of his reign, pride resurfaced in David's heart when he ordered a census of Israel. His confidence had shifted subtly from God's strength to human numbers. Joab, his commander, discerned the error:

"May the LORD your God multiply the troops a hundred times over, and may the eyes of my lord the king see it. But why does my lord the king want to do such a thing?" (2 Samuel 24:3–4, NIV)

David's act provoked judgment, reminding him—and us—that reliance on self is rebellion against grace. Though he repented, this episode underscores that consecration and sacrifice are not once-for-all acts but living disciplines sustained through prayer, Scripture, worship, and fellowship. Human nature drifts toward complacency; maturity resists it. The mature remain vigilant, continually refreshed in spirit.

The Enduring Lesson

David's story is both victory and warning. The journey of becoming never ends. Even at the summit of calling, consecration and sacrifice remain the keys that preserve the anointing. The moment one ceases to yield, the oil begins to dry.

'Becoming' is not an achievement—it is a rhythm of continual surrender. :')

DANIEL, SHADRACH, MESHACH, AND ABEDNEGO: The Impact of Becoming

In *Ezra* 1:1–4, we witness the fulfillment of prophecy and the culmination of God's divine plan through faithful pattern bearers. The passage declares:

"In the first year of Cyrus king of Persia, in order to fulfill the word of the LORD spoken by Jeremiah, the LORD moved the heart of Cyrus king of Persia to make a proclamation throughout his realm and also to put it in writing: "This is what Cyrus king of Persia says:

"'The LORD, the God of heaven, has given me all the kingdoms of the earth and he has appointed me to build a temple for Him at Jerusalem in Judah. Any of His people among you may go up to Jerusalem in Judah and build the temple of the LORD, the God of Israel, the God who is in Jerusalem, and may their God be with them. And in any locality where survivors may now be living, the people are to provide them with silver and gold, with goods and livestock, and with freewill offerings for the temple of God in Jerusalem.'"
(Ezra 1:1–4, NIV)

King Cyrus's acknowledgment of the LORD was not a sudden impulse but the result of a divine sequence—*a chain of testimonies* woven through time and nations. His decree marked the visible outcome of spiritual forces long at work through four faithful men—Daniel, Shadrach, Meshach, and Abednego.

Their witness in Babylon's courts became *international proclamations* of Yahweh's supremacy. Nebuchadnezzar twice declared God's sovereignty—first, when Shadrach, Meshach, and Abednego were delivered from the fiery furnace, and again, when Daniel interpreted his dream, unveiling heaven's authority over kings. Later, Darius the Mede, who served under

Cyrus, issued yet another decree to all nations, affirming that "He is the living God, and His kingdom shall not be destroyed." Each royal declaration became a building block, preparing the heart of Cyrus to recognize the God of Israel.

Thus, when Cyrus finally proclaimed freedom for the exiles, he was responding not to novelty, but to revelation—the cumulative weight of divine testimony through faithful lives.

These men—pattern bearers of consecration, sacrifice, and divine appointment—embodied *the Principle of Becoming*. Their steadfastness in trial and purity under pressure altered the course of empires. Through their obedience, the captivity of Israel was ended, and prophecy fulfilled.

This account reveals a sacred truth: *faithfulness in becoming is never private—it is generational*. When you endure the refining fires, your obedience births deliverance for others. To walk the path of consecration and sacrifice is to steward an inheritance that reaches beyond your lifetime.

As Daniel, Shadrach, Meshach, and Abednego stood firm in Babylon, their witness unlocked divine favor across nations. Likewise, those who remain faithful to the call of becoming will see God use their journey as a bridge for others to enter freedom.

This testimony calls every believer who seeks to follow God's path: **Remain steadfast. Honor the process. Embrace the journey of becoming.** For it is not for your glory alone, but for the glory of God and the salvation of many.

ESTHER AND MORDECAI: The Impact of Becoming

Before we examine Esther, it is fitting to begin with Mordecai's journey—another remarkable pattern bearer who had fully become and stood firm in his divine purpose. After Esther interceded and courageously exposed Haman's evil plot against the Jews, the king fully supported the campaign to preserve God's people. Though the genocidal decree influenced by Haman was irrevocable under Persian law, King Xerxes handed his signet ring to Mordecai, empowering him to write a counter-decree, seal it with the king's authority, and dispatch swift messengers on royal horses throughout the provinces.

Mordecai's life exemplified the three prerequisites of the journey to become. He stood steadfast beside Esther, wielding divine power as a faithful servant of the highest authority in Persia—two mighty pattern bearers preserving God's covenant people from annihilation. Mordecai's consecration shone through his refusal to bow to Haman—an idolatrous act that would have desecrated his devotion to Yahweh alone, the God of Israel. It was an unequivocal statement of spiritual allegiance and purity.

Furthermore, Mordecai demonstrated loyalty and courage when he uncovered a conspiracy by the king's eunuchs to assassinate the monarch. Yet, despite this act of service, he experienced the refining fire of sacrifice—being overlooked and unrewarded for a season, patiently serving at the king's gate with unwavering faithfulness. His refusal to bow to Haman, even after considering the latter's power, tested his obedience and courage under immense pressure. Haman, second only to the king, demanded homage; yet Mordecai risked everything to honor divine truth.

When Haman sought Mordecai's death, God intervened. In a divine reversal, Mordecai was elevated in position and honor, and through Esther's wisdom and bravery, their deliverance was sealed. Together, Esther and Mordecai embodied the fullness of becoming—faithful vessels operating in divine authority to preserve a nation.

The counter-decree issued under Mordecai's seal was proclaimed across all provinces, commanding the Jews to stand ready to defend themselves. The result was jubilation throughout the land:

"In every province and in every city to which the edict of the king came, there was joy and gladness among the Jews, with feasting and celebrating. And many people of other nationalities became Jews because fear of the Jews had seized them." (Esther 8:17, NIV)

This fear and reverence for God's movement among the nations demonstrated the transformative power of those who have become. Their faith compels others to turn toward God and abandon corrupt systems of the world.

Indeed, Scripture records:

"And all the nobles of the provinces, the satraps, the governors and the king's administrators helped the Jews, because fear of Mordecai had seized them." (Esther 9:3, NIV)

Mordecai's rise in influence and fame safeguarded God's people, and their triumph birthed the annual festival of Purim—a lasting memorial of divine preservation through those who fully entered their role in God's redemptive plan.

The Sovereign Impact of Becoming

The stories of Daniel, Shadrach, Meshach, Abednego, Esther, and Mordecai together unveil the sovereign wisdom and providence of God. Despite Israel's exile and repeated unfaithfulness, His plan for restoration remained unbroken. Through divine foresight, God strategically positioned faithful servants within foreign empires to protect His covenant people.

In Babylon, Daniel and his companions held positions of high authority, forming a political and spiritual canopy over the Israelites. Their steadfast witness caused kings to fear and honor the name of Yahweh, ensuring divine protection even in captivity. This canopy of favor was not accidental but instrumental to God's plan, while prophets like Ezekiel ministered to the exiles' hearts, stirring repentance and hope.

God used Daniel's rise—and the spread of reverence for His name among nations—to prepare the way for Israel's eventual restoration. His methods intertwined governance and spirituality, showing that becoming is multi-dimensional. Some are accelerated like Joseph; others are refined slowly like Jacob. Yet all are essential parts of the same divine design.

This blueprint confirms that those who fully become are strategic instruments in God's grand symphony—positioned to influence nations and advance His Kingdom.

Therefore, let this be your call and charge: **Embrace the journey of becoming.** Dedicate yourself to consecration. Endure the fires of sacrifice. Prepare for divine appointment.

For as the Lord Jesus declared, *"The harvest truly is plentiful, but the laborers are few. Therefore pray to the LORD of the harvest to send out laborers into His harvest."* *(Matthew 9:37, NKJV)*

When you have 'become,' you are empowered to fulfill God's purpose, bring salvation to many, and live a life of true and eternal impact.

NEW TESTAMENT PATTERN BEARERS: The Fulfillment of The Journey to Become

JESUS: **The Fulfillment of the Journey to Become**

After emerging from the wilderness experience—His sacrifice prerequisite—Jesus returned in the power of the Spirit. He cast out demons, healed the sick, raised the dead, and taught with authority about the Kingdom of God. Multitudes flocked to Him, sustained by His miracles and strengthened by His message of hope. Jesus brought light to those oppressed under Roman rule and offered life to the hopeless. He became *the embodiment of divine becoming*, surpassing any human example one could conceive.

Jesus modeled the principles of consecration and sacrifice perfectly. Compassion marked His every act; prayer marked His every morning. He rose early to commune with the Father, living in total consecration and surrender to the One who sent Him. Though the demands of His mission were great, He cultivated margin—often withdrawing to pray—teaching us the necessity of personal devotion amid public ministry.

At the culmination of His journey, as a perfected Pattern Bearer, Jesus gave His life for the salvation of the world. Scripture declares: *"He was pierced for our transgressions, he was crushed for our iniquities; the punishment that brought us peace was on him, and by his wounds we are healed...He was assigned a grave with the wicked...though he had done no violence, nor was any deceit in his mouth."* (Isaiah 53:5–9, NIV)

Though the Son of God, He clothed Himself in humility. Even as He endured crucifixion, He interceded in loving maturity for His executioners, praying: *"Father, forgive them, for they do not know what they are doing."* (Luke 23:34, NIV)

His compassion extended to His human responsibilities even unto death; He entrusted His mother's care to His beloved disciple John (*John 19:26–27*), revealing the perfect balance of divine mission and tender humanity.

With arms stretched wide upon the cross, Jesus declared the triumphant words: *"It is finished."* (John 19:30)

He completed His purpose—dying and rising three days later to conquer sin and death. After His resurrection, He commissioned His apostles and ascended to the right hand of the Father, where He continually intercedes for us: *"Therefore he is able to save completely those who come to God through him, because he always lives to intercede for them."* (Hebrews 7:25, NIV)

THE DISCIPLES: Emulating the Master in Power and Spirit

The disciples—Peter, John, James, and the rest—fully embraced the journey to become, emulating their Master in both character and power. Before the Sanhedrin, their fearless testimony astonished the rulers, who recognized them as *"unschooled men"* who had been with Jesus (*Acts 4:13, NIV*).

After completing their sacrifice prerequisite—culminating at Pentecost—they walked in Christ's likeness and power openly. The early church experienced unprecedented revival, spreading the gospel with force and conviction.

They were first called *"the people of the Way,"* and later, *"Christians."* The very shadow of Peter healed the sick (*Acts 5:15*), a visible sign of divine endorsement upon their ministry. They saw visions, performed wonders, and raised the dead—Dorcas being one such miracle, raised by Peter (*Acts 9:36–42*).

These signs and wonders were the fruits of the journey to become—rooted firmly in divine appointment. Among them was Stephen, the first Christian martyr, who embodied profound loving-maturity. As stones rained upon him, he prayed with grace: *"Lord, do not hold this sin against them."* (Acts 7:60, NIV)

The New Testament writers themselves were the product of this same journey. The beloved apostle John, through revelation from the risen Christ, authored the Book of Revelation, unveiling eternal truths to strengthen and warn the Church.

All of this flows from the principle of becoming—a divine, non-negotiable journey for every believer called to spiritual leadership and Kingdom service. It is the pathway that equips and empowers us to fulfill the Great Commission and manifest our God-ordained purpose as His Church.

THE LIFE OF APOSTLE PAUL: The Culmination of the Journey to Become

Having arrived at his final prerequisite—the place of divine appointment—Apostle Paul embodied the principle of becoming in its most complete form. His life bore unwavering dedication to the divine purpose assigned to him by Jesus Christ. As Paul himself declared:

"I consider my life worth nothing to me; my only aim is to finish the race and complete the task the Lord Jesus has given me—the task of testifying to the good news of God's grace." (Acts 20:24, NIV)

Paul's singular pursuit was to fulfill God's calling through faithful service and sacrifice. This was no mere confession but a deep conviction that defined his being. He affirmed this truth again when he wrote: *"For to me, to live is Christ and to die is gain."* (Philippians 1:21, NIV) and, *"I have been crucified with Christ and I no longer live, but Christ lives in me."* (Galatians 2:20, NIV)

His life was continually marked by consecration and sacrifice to God's will. Paul did not mourn his mortal frailty; rather, he embraced it as essential to his divine journey. Having laid down all that once held him dear, even before his salvation, he boldly testified:

"What is more, I consider everything a loss because of the surpassing worth of knowing Christ Jesus my Lord, for whose sake I have lost all things. I consider

them rubbish, that I may gain Christ." (Philippians 3:8, NIV) His boast was never in himself, but in Christ who transformed him.

Loving-Maturity Exemplified in Paul

Paul's loving-maturity radiated through his acceptance of weakness for the manifestation of divine strength. He records in 2 Corinthians 12:9–10:

"But he said to me, 'My grace is sufficient for you, for my power is made perfect in weakness.' Therefore I will boast all the more gladly about my weaknesses, so that Christ's power may rest on me. That is why, for Christ's sake, I delight in weaknesses, in insults, in hardships, in persecutions, in difficulties. For when I am weak, then I am strong." (NIV)

His love was so profound that, like Moses, he was willing to forfeit his own salvation if it meant the redemption of his people, Israel. This deep intercessory compassion is revealed in Romans 9:3:

"For I could wish that I myself were cursed and cut off from Christ for the sake of my people, those of my own race." (NIV)

This rare love mirrors Moses' selfless plea for Israel's forgiveness, embodying the same heart of divine maturity that stands in the gap for a rebellious people, bearing their burden in prayer and compassion.

Paul's consecration was further evidenced when, compelled by the Spirit, he journeyed to Jerusalem despite prophetic warnings of imprisonment. Though others pleaded for him to turn back, his submission to God's will was absolute. He declared:

"I consider my life worth nothing to me; my only aim is to finish the race and complete the task the Lord Jesus has given me—the task of testifying to the good news of God's grace." (Acts 20:24, NIV)

Even after entering the realm of divine appointment, Paul remained steadfast, counting all worldly gain as loss for the excellence of knowing Christ (*Philippians 3:8*). His entire existence was poured out as an offering of obedience and love.

Paul's life stands as the vivid conclusion to our study of biblical pattern bearers—the last and suitably complete example of the journey to become. His transformative faith, relentless consecration, sacrificial devotion, and triumphant walk in divine appointment reveal the profound truth: *to become is to be wholly set apart for God's purposes.*

Such a life shapes destiny, influences generations, and fulfills divine intention. This is the timeless call of every believer entrusted with the Great Commission—to walk fully in the principle of becoming, empowered to fulfill God's redemptive plan on the earth.

THE KINGDOM OF GOD: THE POWER AND PURPOSE OF BECOMING

The Kingdom of God is fundamentally a demonstration of power, not mere words. As Paul declares: *"For the kingdom of God is not a matter of talk but of power."* (1 Corinthians 4:20, NIV)

This divine reality is vividly displayed in the lives of the biblical pattern bearers we have studied. Though each story differs, all follow the same sacred sequence—*consecration, sacrifice,* and *divine appointment:* the journey to *becoming.* The expression of this power may vary—some are called to spiritual ministry, others to realms of governance, commerce, law, or defense—but the constant remains faithfulness to God's calling and endurance through the process.

Abraham's becoming birthed a nation through which salvation would come. Jacob, transformed into Israel, became the father of tribes through whom God preserved the lineage of the Messiah. Joseph's becoming preserved Israel in famine, preparing Egypt as the womb of a nation. Moses became deliverer, leading God's people from bondage to sovereignty. David secured their borders and established the eternal royal line through which Christ would come. Esther's courage delivered her generation from annihilation.

Even before Abraham's time, the Principle of Becoming was already evident in the life of Noah. Set apart from his generation, God recognized him as the only righteous man in the entire world at that time. Noah fulfilled the requirements of the first prerequisite—**Primal Consecration**. Because of this consecration, God called him and entrusted him with an assignment. This marked the entry into the second prerequisite—the place of **Sacrifice**, where responsibility is tested and obedience is proven.

Noah burned through this prerequisite with unwavering faithfulness. Using his own resources, he built the ark exactly as God had instructed him, despite the ridicule and sentiments of the people around him. For one hundred and twenty years he labored and preached to a sinful world, warning them of the coming flood. This long season of labor, endurance, and faithful proclamation was sacrifice in its purest form.

At last, the transition into his final prerequisite came in the form of the great flood. With the animals safely within the ark and his family preserved, Noah entered the stage of **Divine Appointment**. His obedience had brought him into the fullness of the purpose for which God had created him. When the waters receded and the ark rested upon the mountain ranges of Ararat, Noah's family multiplied, preserving the human race. The animals also multiplied, filling the earth once again.

Had Noah not remained faithful in this early and powerful example of the Principle of Becoming, the entire human race would have been lost to the deluge. Through consecration, sacrifice, and divine appointment, Noah became exactly what God had intended—a vessel through whom the future of humanity was preserved.

And greater than all, Jesus Christ—the perfect Pattern Bearer—fulfilled every prerequisite to become our ultimate Redeemer. He walked the road of consecration, sacrifice, and divine appointment, that through His death and resurrection we might attain eternal life. Scripture declares:

"He who did not spare his own Son but gave him up for us all—how will he not also, along with him, graciously give us all things?" (Romans 8:32, NIV)and again,

"For you know the grace of our Lord Jesus Christ, that though he was rich, yet for your sake he became poor, so that you through his poverty might become rich." (2 Corinthians 8:9, NIV)

Every act of becoming in Scripture serves one ultimate purpose: *the salvation of souls.* Christ's suffering and sacrifice satisfied divine justice, opening the way for humanity's redemption.

Thus, to understand the *Principle of Becoming* is to navigate destiny with clarity and precision—to fulfill divine purpose in its highest measure. For God's desire is that none should perish but that all come to the saving knowledge of truth (*1 Timothy 2:3–4*). When we embrace this journey, we become instruments of His redemptive plan—vessels of power transforming lives and generations. *(2 Timothy 2:21)*

This is the Kingdom of God in operation—the power alive within those who dare to *become*.

There Are No Shortcuts in the Crucible

Shortcuts in the journey to *become* are never within God's will. They are detours laid by the enemy to divert the called from destiny. Even Jesus was offered a false shortcut in the wilderness:

"The devil took him to a very high mountain and showed him all the kingdoms of the world and their splendor. 'All this I will give you,' he said, 'if you will bow down and worship me.'" (Matthew 4:8–9, NIV)

But Jesus refused the shortcut. He chose the Father's will—to drink the appointed cup, endure the cross, descend into death, and rise victorious over sin and Hades. Only through obedience, suffering, and resurrection—the long and narrow road of the crucible—did He inherit the name above every name (*Philippians 2:8–11*).

This is the divine pattern—the Principle of Becoming. Christ endured the process not for self-glory, but for the redemption of souls. Every pattern bearer, as we have seen, journeys through the same refining fire—not for self-promotion, but for the salvation and deliverance of others.

"For those God foreknew he also predestined to be conformed to the image of his Son, that he might be the firstborn among many brothers and sisters." (Romans 8:29, NIV)

If the Father did not spare His own Son from the fire, He will not exempt those called to advance His Kingdom. His love for souls is too great to permit half-formed vessels or negligent stewards. Thus, Jesus warns: *"Whoever wants to be my disciple must deny themselves and take up their cross daily and follow me."* (Luke 9:23, NIV)

Burn through your crucible with courage and resolve, for the glory that awaits outweighs every moment of trial. The King will not jeopardize the destinies of many for the comfort of one. Either rise, take your place in the making, or be replaced. The principle stands immutable: the process is the path to power; the fire is the womb of divine authority.

The glory in the end will make every season of testing worth it.

Arise. Embrace the call. Become.

'Après moi, la gloire!'

THE PRINCIPLE OF BECOMING

CLARION CALL

The Burden of Knowledge: The Weight of Responsibility

The burden of knowledge is the weight of responsibility that follows it. Now that you grasp the journey—the arduous content, the fulfilling rewards, and the fullness awaiting at its end—it becomes your solemn responsibility to carry the weight of this journey. The path to *becoming* is not merely knowledge; it is the crucible of action, dedication, and transformation.

I implore you: accept the will of the LORD for your life. Deep within, we all desire to *become*, but few are truly prepared to embrace the process. We yearn for the splendor without enduring the refining fires. You cannot cheat God's divine systems. The journey demands consecration, sacrifice, and steadfastness. It requires humility, perseverance, and trust.

As highlighted in the introduction, this principle belongs to the precious few—about one percent of biblical truths—that can only be genuinely applied after the prerequisite of salvation. You cannot embark on the journey of becoming if you have not been born again; to try otherwise is chasing after the wind. All the pattern bearers we have studied were God's chosen, His ordained vessels who submitted wholeheartedly, in obedience and reverence, to the divine process.

The Word reassures us of God's faithful mercy and unending compassion: *"Because of the LORD's great love we are not consumed, for his compassions never fail. They are new every morning; great is your faithfulness. I say to myself, 'The LORD is my portion; therefore I will wait for him.' The LORD is good to those whose hope is in him, to the one who seeks him."* (Lamentations 3:22–25, NIV)

A Prayer of Surrender to Begin the Journey

"Dear Heavenly Father,

I have walked this life unaware of the fullness of Your calling, uncertain of Your requirements. Where fear has held me back, where comfort has lulled me, I now surrender completely. Free me from hesitation and doubt. Guide my steps and make my path clear, so I shall not stumble. I believe; help my unbelief. Strengthen and build me up, Abba Father. I yield all—my heart, my will, my life—to You. I accept Christ's sacrifice as payment for my sins and embrace the new life You give through Him. I confess with my mouth, believe with my heart, and declare that I am born again. Amen."

Having prayed in faith, believe it: you are born again, for *"If you declare with your mouth, 'Jesus is Lord,' and believe in your heart that God raised him from the dead, you will be saved."* (Romans 10:9, NIV)

A Prayer to Launch the Journey of Becoming

"Abba Father,

Glory be to Your holy name above all else. I come as Your child, eager and ready to journey through the prerequisites toward divine appointment. I acknowledge my human weakness and declare that this journey is only possible by Your Holy Spirit's power. Guide me; hold me fast; lead me in the way everlasting. Though the unknown ahead may cause fear, I choose to trust You fully. Launch me into this journey—consecration, sacrifice, and steady faithfulness. Strengthen me and fill me with courage. In Jesus' name, Amen."

Now, receive this blessing:

"The LORD bless you and keep you; the LORD make His face shine upon you and be gracious to you; the LORD lift up His countenance upon you and give you peace." (Numbers 6:24–26, NKJV)

As He was with Shadrach, Meshach, and Abednego in the fiery furnace—preserving them without even the smell of smoke upon their garments—may He be with you always. May you excel through all the prerequisites, ascend in power, and steward your influence rightly.

The King will one day proclaim to you: *"Well done, good and faithful servant... Enter into the joy of your Lord."* (Matthew 25:23, NKJV)

SHALOM and MARANATHA,

Christ's Faithful Vassal,

JEHU :')

About the author

Yeshua S. Jehu, authors the five-book *Shepherd's Pouch* series. Tailored for believers, it tackles power, financial stewardship, wealth-building, destiny fulfillment, spiritual development, and sexual purity—equipping you to stand strong in integrity, mature in truth for leadership, discipleship, relationships, and personal life.

The Principle of Becoming, the third installment of the *Shepherd's Pouch* series, unveils the transformative journey of identity, process, and divine alignment. Moving beyond stewardship and strategy, this volume calls believers into the disciplined pursuit of spiritual formation, character refinement, and purposeful evolution.

Through revelatory insight and practical wisdom, it introduces original frameworks that cultivate maturity, resilience, and intentional growth—equipping readers to embrace the process of becoming who God has ordained them to be, and to walk boldly in destiny with clarity, integrity, and power.

Interconnected yet standalone, each volume ensures you grow fully equipped, lacking nothing.

Connect with the Author

Follow me on social media to stay updated:

Twitter/X: @Yeshua_S_Jehu

Instagram: @Yeshua_S_Jehu

LinkedIn: @Yeshua Jehu

Stay connected—discover new updates, behind-the-scenes stories, and keep the conversation going. Connect, share, and be part of the journey.

The Shepherd's Pouch: A Five-Book Vision for Biblical Dominion

The Shepherd's Pouch is the visionary name of this transformative five-book series, with *The Principle of Becoming* serving as the compelling third installment. This volume shifts the focus from external pillars of power to the internal architecture of identity—revealing that before influence is sustained or wealth is multiplied, the individual must be forged.

It equips you with revelatory wisdom for spiritual formation, character refinement, and disciplined growth, unveiling the essential process that prepares a believer to carry power with integrity and endurance.

That profound progression continues through Books 4–5, each delivered with the same consistent excellence—interconnected as a cohesive series, yet individually complete, satisfying, and independent.

Book 1 opened the door to managing influence and power with purity and divine cunning. Book 2 unlocked the first pillar: Finances/Wealth. *The Principle of Becoming* now establishes the indispensable growth process that upholds every pillar with divine integrity—identity, transformation, and the intentional process of becoming who you are divinely designed to be.

These are the three pillars of human society from which dominion over the earth becomes possible through God's divinely set principles—pillars upon which this entire series teaches passionately: **Sexuality, Religion/Spirituality,** and **Finances/Wealth.**

These are the roots of dominion, power, and influence, without which the church cannot wield transformative power for divine effect. Discover how these pillars are rooted in Scripture, first revealed in Genesis 1:28 as the eternal formula for power, as you journey through the entirety of this series.

Experience the *"fruitfulness"* of true spiritual life that pleases God and re-shapes society; the divine *"multiplication"* born from the purity of sexuality, radiating righteous integrity across every avenue of life; the knowledge to build wealth that empowers you to *"subdue"* the earth and enact physical change with authority; and finally, the *"dominion"* that manifests as you master these three pillars through the wisdom and revelation of the Holy Spirit—applied with unshakable practicality.

"Then God blessed them, and God said to them, 'Be fruitful and multiply; fill the earth and subdue it; have dominion over the fish of the sea, over the birds of the air, and over every living thing that moves on the earth.'" (Genesis 1:28, NKJV)

Unlock the complete series and step into your divine authority. God bless you!

Also by Yeshua S. Jehu

THE SHEPHERD'S POUCH Series

Book 1: The 48 Laws of Power Biblically

Book 2: Money Biblically

Book 3: The Principle of Becoming

Book 4: The Five Guardians of Spiritual Fervour

Book 5: Purity Rises from Above

"Dare to complete the pouch? Interlock power, influence, purity, and spiritual vitality—unlock their divine interconnectivity. *Hope to see you in the next volume, fully armed." :')*